Canadian Legal Forms & Agreements

C.G.T. Canadian Legal Forms Ltd
Burnaby, B.C.
service@CanadaForms.com

> **NOTICE:**
>
> THIS PRODUCT IS NOT INTENDED TO PROVIDE LEGAL ADVICE. IT CONTAINS GENERAL INFORMATION FOR EDUCATIONAL PURPOSES ONLY. PLEASE CONSULT A LAWYER ABOUT ALL LEGAL MATTERS. THIS PRODUCT WAS NOT NECESSARILY PREPARED BY A PERSON LICENSED TO PRACTICE LAW IN YOUR PROVINCE.

Canadian Legal Forms and Agreements
© Copyright 2001   C.G.T. Canadian Legal Forms Ltd
P.O. Box 82664
Burnaby, B.C. V5C 5W4
service@CanadaForms.com
All rights reserved.

1 2 3 4 5 6 7 8 9 10

This publication is designed to provide accurate and authoritative information in regard to subject matter covered. It is sold with the understanding that neither the publisher nor author is engaged in rendering legal, accounting, or other professional services. If legal advice or other expert assistance is required, the services of a competent professional should be sought.

Canadian Legal Forms and Agreements

Important Notice

This product is intended for informational use only and is not a substitute for legal advice. Provincial laws vary and change, and the information or forms do not necessarily conform to the laws or requirements of your province. While you always have the right to prepare your own documents and to act as your own lawyer, do consult a lawyer on all important legal matters. This product was not necessarily prepared by a person licensed to practice law in your province.

Limited warranty and disclaimer

This self-help product is intended to be used by the consumer for his/her own benefit. It may not be reproduced in whole or in part, resold or used for commercial purposes without written permission from the publisher. In addition to copyright violations, the unauthorized reproduction and use of this product to benefit a second party may be considered the unauthorized practice of law.

This product is designed to provide authoritative and accurate information in regard to the subject matter covered. However, the accuracy of the information is not guaranteed, as laws and regulations may change or be subject to differing interpretations. Consequently, you may be responsible for following alternative procedures, or using material or forms different from those supplied with this product. It is strongly advised that you examine the laws of your province before acting upon any of the material contained in this product.

As with any matter, common sense should determine whether you need the assistance of a lawyer. We urge you to consult with a lawyer, qualified estate planner, or tax professional, or to seek any other relevant expert advice whenever substantial sums of money are involved, you doubt the suitability of the product you have purchased, or if there is anything about the product that you do not understand including its adequacy to protect you. Even if you are completely satisfied with this product, we encourage you to have your lawyer review it.

Neither the author, publisher, distributor nor retailer are engaged in rendering legal, accounting or other professional services. Accordingly, the publisher, author, distributor and retailer shall have neither liability nor responsibility to any party for any loss or damage caused or alleged to be caused by the use of this product.

Copyright Notice

The purchaser of this guide is hereby authorized to reproduce in any form or by any means, electronic or mechanical, including photocopying, all forms and documents contained in this guide, provided it is for non-profit, educational or private use. Such reproduction requires no further permission from the publisher and/or payment of any permission fee.

The reproduction of any form or document in any other publication intended for sale is prohibited without the written permission of the publisher. Publication for nonprofit use should provide proper attribution to C.G.T. Canadian Legal Forms Ltd.

How to use this guide

    C.G.T. Canadian Legal Forms Ltd Guides can help you achieve an important legal objective conveniently, efficiently and economically. But it is important to properly use this guide if you are to avoid later difficulties.

- ◆ Carefully read all information, warnings and disclaimers concerning the legal forms in this guide. If after thorough examination you decide that you have circumstances that are not covered by the forms in this guide, or you do not feel confident about preparing your own documents, consult a lawyer.

- ◆ Complete each blank on each legal form. Do not skip over inapplicable blanks or lines intended to be completed. If the blank is inapplicable, mark "N/A" or "None" or use a dash. This shows you have not overlooked the item.

- ◆ Always use pen or type on legal documents—never use pencil.

- ◆ Avoid erasures and "cross-outs" on final documents. Use photocopies of each document as worksheets, or as final copies. All documents submitted to the court must be printed on one side only.

- ◆ Correspondence forms may be reproduced on your own letterhead if you prefer.

- ◆ Whenever legal documents are to be executed by a partnership or corporation, the signatory should designate his or her title.

- ◆ It is important to remember that on legal contracts or agreements between parties all terms and conditions must be clearly stated. Provisions may not be enforccable unless in writing. All parties to the agreement should receive a copy.

- ◆ Instructions contained in this guide are for your benefit and protection, so follow them closely.

- ◆ Always keep legal documents in a safe place and in a location known to your spouse, family, personal representative or lawyer.

TABLE OF CONTENTS
Alphabetical

—A—

Absence Request 1
Acceptance of Claim 2
Accident Claim Notice 4
Accident Report 5
Acknowledged Receipt of Goods 6
Acknowledgement of Modified Terms 7
Acknowledgement of Temporary Employment 8
Addendum to Contract 9
Addendum to Employment Agreement 10
Address Change Notice 11
Agreement of Waiver of Right of Inheritance 12
Agreement on Proprietary Rights 13
Agreement Reminder 15
Agreement to Accept Night Work 16
Agreement to Assume Debt 17
Agreement to Compromise Debt 18
Agreement to Extend Debt Payment 19
Agreement to Extend Performance Date 20
Agreement to Extend Period of Option 21
Agreement to Lease 22
Agreement to Purchase Stock 24
Agreement to Sell Personal Property 25
Amendment to Lease 26
Analysis of Cash Available for Debt Repayment 27
Applicant Acknowledgement 28
Applicant Interview Confirmation 29
Applicant Notification 30
Applicant Referral Program 31
Applicant Waiver 32
Assignment by Endorsing on Lease 33
Assignment of Accounts Receivable with Non-Recourse 34
Assignment of Accounts Receivable with Recourse 35
Assignment of Assets 36
Assignment of Bank Account 37
Assignment of Contract 38
Assignment of Damage Claim 39

Table of Contents

Assignment of Income 40
Assignment of Insurance Policy 41
Assignment of Lease 42
Assignment of Money Due 44
Assignment of Option 45
Authorization to Release Confidential Information 46
Authorization to Release Credit Information 47
Authorization to Release Employment Information 48
Authorization to Release Financial Statements 49
Authorization to Release Information 50
Authorization to Release Medical Information 51
Authorization to Return Goods 52

—B—

Bad Cheque Notice 53
Balloon Note 54
Bill of Sale 55
Breach of Contract Notice 56

—C—

Cancellation of Stop-Payment Order 57
Certificate of Corporate Resolution 58
Change of Beneficiary 59
Change Work Order 60
Cheque Stop-Payment 61
Child Guardianship Consent Form 62
Cohabitation Agreement 63
Commercial Lease 65
Confidentiality Agreement 69
Confirmation of Verbal Agreement 71
Confirmation of Verbal Order 72
Conflict of Interest Declaration 73
Consent for Drug/Alcohol Screen Testing 74
Consent to Assignment 75
Consent to Partial Assignment 76
Consent to Release of Information 77
Consignment Agreement 78
Consulting Services Agreement 80
Contract 81
Credit Information Request 82
Credit Interchange 83

VII

Canadian Legal Forms and Agreements

—D—

Declaration of Trust 84
Defective Goods Notice..85
Demand for Contribution 86
Demand for Delivery..87
Demand for Payment 1 88
Demand for Payment 2 89
Demand for Payment 3 90
Demand for Payment 4 91
Demand for Rent...92
Demand on Guarantor 93
Demand on Guarantor for Payment 94
Demand Promissory Note 95
Demand to Endorser for Payment...96
Demand to Pay Promissory Note 97
Direct Deposit Authorization 98
Disciplinary Notice 99
Dishonored Cheque Placed for Bank Collection 100
Disputed Account Settlement 101

—E—

Employee Agreement on Inventions and Patents..102
Employee Checkout Record 104
Employee Consultation..105
Employee Covenant: Expense Recovery 106
Employee Exit Interview..107
Employee Indemnity Agreement 109
Employee Information Update 110
Employee Non-Compete Agreement 111
Employee Non-Disclosure Agreement 112
Employee Referral Request..113
Employee Release...114
Employee Salary Record 115
Employee Warning...116
Employee's Agreement on Confidential Data..117
Employment Agreement..118
Employment Application 121
Employment Application Disclaimer and Acknowledgement 123
Employment Changes 124
Exceptions to Purchase Order 125
Exclusive Right to Sell 126
Exercise of Option 128

Table of Contents

Extended Term Rescinded and Demand for Payment 129
Extension of Agreement 130
Extension of Debt Payment Agreement 131
Extension of Lease 132

—F—

Final Notice Before Legal Action 133
Final Warning Before Dismissal 134
First Warning Notice 135
Funeral Leave Request 136

—G—

General Agreement 137
General Assignment 139
General Nondisclosure Agreement 140
General Subordination 141
Grant of Right to Use Name 142
Grievance Form 143
Guaranty 145
Guaranty of Rents 147

—H—

Help Wanted Advertising Listing 148

—I—

Illness Report 149
Incident Report 150
Indemnity Agreement 151
Independent Contractor Agreement 152
Information Request on Disputed Charges 153
Injury Report 154
Insurance Claim Notice 155
Invitation to Quote Price of Goods 156

—L—

Landlord's and Tenant's Mutual Release 157
Landlord's Notice to Terminate Tenancy 158
Landlord's Notice to Vacate 159
Last Will and Testament 160
Lease Termination Agreement 162

Canadian Legal Forms and Agreements

Leave Request/Return from Leave 163
Letter of Commendation...164
Letter Requesting Authorization to Release Credit Information 165
Limited Guaranty...166
List of Shareholders 167
Lost Credit Card Notice 168

—M—

Mailing List Name Removal Request 169
Minutes of Annual Meeting of Stockholders..170
Minutes of Combined Meeting of Stockholders and Directors..................................172
Minutes of Directors' Meeting 174
Minutes of First Meeting of Shareholders 175
Minutes of Special Meeting of Stockholders..177
Mutual Cancellation of Contract 179
Mutual Releases 180

—N—

New Employee Data..181
No Decision on Hiring 182
Non-Compete Agreement 183
Non-Disclosure of Trade Secrets 184
Notice of 30-day Evaluation 185
Notice of Annual Shareholders' Meeting..186
Notice of Assignment...187
Notice of Assignment to Obligor..188
Notice of Available Position 189
Notice of C.O.D. Terms 190
Notice of Cash-Only Terms 191
Notice of Change in Rent...192
Notice of Confidentiality Agreement 193
Notice of Corrected Account 194
Notice of Debt Assignment..195
Notice of Default in Payment 196
Notice of Default on Extension Agreement 197
Notice of Default on Promissory Note..198
Notice of Dismissal 199
Notice of Disputed Account 200
Notice of Election to Cancel...201
Notice of Forfeiture...202
Notice of Intent to Repossess Due to Default 203
Notice of Probation 204

Notice of Rent Arrears..205
Notice of Results of Public Sale...206
Notice of Termination Due to Absence..207
Notice of Termination Due to Work Rules Violation..208
Notice of Unpaid Invoice...209
Notice of Waiver of Annual Meeting By All Shareholders..210
Notice of Wrongful Refusal to Accept Delivery..211
Notice to Cancel Back-Ordered Goods...212
Notice to Cancel Delayed Goods...213
Notice to Creditor to Pay Specific Accounts..214
Notice to Directors of Special Meeting...215
Notice to Exercise Lease Option..216
Notice to Landlord to Make Repairs...217
Notice to Officer of Removal From Board..218
Notice to Purchaser of Breach of Option..219
Notice to Reclaim Goods..220
Notice to Redirect Payments..221
Notice to Re-issue Cheque..222
Notice to Remedy Default by Tenant..223
Notice to Shareholders of Annual Meeting..224
Notice to Stop Credit Charge...225
Notice to Stop Goods in Transit...226
Notice to Tenant to Make Repairs...227

—O—

Option to Purchase...228
Option to Purchase Stock...229

—P—

Partial Shipment Request...230
Past Due Reminder...231
Payment Inquiry..232
Payment on Specific Accounts...233
Payment on Written Instrument..234
Payments to a Creditor...235
Permission to Use Copyrighted Material...236
Permission to Use Quote or Personal Statement...237
Personal Property Rental Agreement...238
Personnel Data Change..239
Personnel Data Sheet..240
Preliminary Employment Application...241
Presentment by Mail...242

Privacy Release 243
Product Defect Claim 244
Product Defect Notice 245
Product Warranty Claim 246
Promissory Note 247
Proposal to Buy a Business 249
Purchase Requirement Agreement 250
Purchaser's Assignment of Option 251

—R—

Receipt 252
Receipt for Balance of Account 253
Receipt for Company Property 254
Receipt in Full by an Agent 255
Receipt in Full by an Agent to an Agent 256
Receipt of Note for Collection 257
Receipt on Account for Goods to be Delivered 258
Receipt on Account for Partial Payment 259
Reference Report 260
Release of Breach of Lease by Tenant 261
Release—Individual 262
Renewal of Notice of Assignment of Accounts 263
Reply to Applicant 264
Request for Bank Credit Reference 265
Request for Credit Interchange 266
Request for Information on Overdue Account 267
Request for Prepayment 268
Request for Reference 269
Request for Transcript 270
Request to Inspect Personnel File 271
Request to Reduce Balance 272
Residential Rental Application 273
Resignation 274
Resume Acknowledgement 275
Retirement Checklist 276
Return of Claim as Noncollectible 277
Revocation of Guaranty 278

—S—

Sale on Approval Acknowledgement 279
Sales Representative Agreement 280
Sample Letter Requesting an Out-of-Court Settlement 282
Sample Letter Requesting Installment Payments 283

Table of Contents

Samples and Documents Receipt...284
Schedule of Assets for Sale or Loan..285
Second Notice of Overdue Account..286
Second Warning Notice..287
Settlement of Disputed Account..288
Settlement Offer on Disputed Account..289
Sight Draft..290
Specific Guaranty..291
Specific Release...292
Statement of Wishes...293
Stock Subscription..294
Sublease..295
Summary of Employment Terms..297
Suspension Without Pay Notice...298

—T—

Temporary Employment Requisition...299
Tenant's Notice to Exercise Purchase Option...300
Tenant's Notice to Terminate Tenancy..301
Termination Checklist..302
Termination Letter for Excessive Absenteeism..303
Termination Letter for Intoxication on the Job..304
Time Note..305
Transmittal for Collection..306
Trip Permission...307

—U—

Unsolicited Idea Acknowledgement..308

—V—

Verification of Education...310
Verification of Employment..311
Verification of Licensure..312

—W—

Waiver and Assumption of Risk..313
Waiver of Liability..314
Waiver of Notice of Annual Meeting by Individual Shareholder...315
Waiver of Notice of Directors' Meeting..316

Waiver of Notice of Organization Meeting of Incorporators and Directors..........................317
Waiver of Notice—Combined Meeting..318
Warranty Bill of Sale 319
Withheld Delivery Notice 320
Written Unanimous Consent in Lieu of Meeting 321

Categorical

I. Basic Agreements
Acceptance of Claim 2
Addendum to Contract 9
Agreement of Waiver of Right of Inheritance 12
Agreement to Extend Performance Date 20
Agreement to Extend Period of Option 21
Agreement to Purchase Stock 24
Agreement to Sell Personal Property 25
Change Work Order 60
Consignment Agreement 78
Consulting Services Agreement 80
Contract 81
Extension of Agreement 130
General Agreement 137
Indemnity Agreement 151
Independent Contractor Agreement 152
Mutual Cancellation of Contract 179
Permission to Use Copyrighted Material 236
Permission to Use Quote or Personal Statement 237
Sales Representative Agreement 280

II. Loans & Borrowing
Agreement to Assume Debt 17
Balloon Note 54
Demand Promissory Note 95
Demand to Endorser for Payment 96
Demand to Pay Promissory Note 97
Guaranty 145
Letter Requesting Authorization to Release Credit Information 165
Limited Guaranty 166
Notice of Default in Payment 196

Notice of Default on Extension Agreement 197
Notice of Default on Promissory Note..198
Notice to Redirect Payments 221
Promissory Note...247
Receipt 252
Receipt for Balance of Account 253
Receipt in Full by an Agent 255
Receipt in Full by an Agent to an Agent..256
Revocation of Guaranty 278
Sight Draft...290
Specific Guaranty 291
Time Note..305

III. Employment

Absence Request 1
Acknowledgement of Temporary Employment..8
Addendum to Employment Agreement..10
Agreement to Accept Night Work 16
Applicant Acknowledgement 28
Applicant Interview Confirmation...29
Applicant Notification...30
Applicant Referral Program 31
Applicant Waiver 32
Authorization to Release Employment Information 48
Authorization to Release Information 50
Confidentiality Agreement...69
Conflict of Interest Declaration 73
Consent for Drug/Alcohol Screen Testing 74
Consent to Release of Information 77
Disciplinary Notice 99
Employee Agreement on Inventions and Patents..102
Employee Checkout Record 104
Employee Consultation...105
Employee Covenant: Expense Recovery 106
Employee Exit Interview...107
Employee Indemnity Agreement 109
Employee Information Update 110
Employee Non-Compete Agreement 111
Employee Non-Disclosure Agreement 112
Employee Referral Request 113
Employee Release..114
Employee Salary Record 115
Employee Warning..116
Employee's Agreement on Confidential Data 117

Employment Agreement 118
Employment Application 121
Employment Application Disclaimer and Acknowledgement 123
Employment Changes 124
Final Warning Before Dismissal 134
First Warning Notice 135
Funeral Leave Request 136
General Nondisclosure Agreement 140
Grievance Form 143
Help Wanted Advertising Listing 148
Illness Report 149
Incident Report 150
Injury Report 154
Leave Request/Return from Leave 163
New Employee Data 181
No Decision on Hiring 182
Non-Compete Agreement 183
Non-Disclosure of Trade Secrets 184
Notice of 30-day Evaluation 185
Notice of Available Position 189
Notice of Confidentiality Agreement 193
Notice of Dismissal 199
Notice of Probation 204
Notice of Termination Due to Absence 207
Notice of Termination Due to Work Rules Violation 208
Personnel Data Change 239
Personnel Data Sheet 240
Preliminary Employment Application 241
Receipt for Company Property 254
Reference Report 260
Reply to Applicant 264
Request for Transcript 270
Request to Inspect Personnel File 271
Resignation 274
Resume Acknowledgement 275
Retirement Checklist 276
Second Warning Notice 287
Summary of Employment Terms 297
Suspension Without Pay Notice 298
Temporary Employment Requisition 299
Termination Checklist 302
Termination Letter for Excessive Absenteeism 303
Termination Letter for Intoxication on the Job 304
Verification of Education 310

Verification of Employment 311
Verification of Licensure 312

IV. Credit & Collection

Agreement to Compromise Debt 18
Agreement to Extend Debt Payment 19
Analysis of Cash Available for Debt Repayment 27
Authorization to Release Credit Information 47
Authorization to Release Financial Statements 49
Cancellation of Stop-Payment Order 57
Credit Information Request 82
Credit Interchange 83
Demand for Payment 1 88
Demand for Payment 2 89
Demand for Payment 3 90
Demand for Payment 4 91
Demand on Guarantor 93
Demand on Guarantor for Payment 94
Disputed Account Settlement 101
Extended Term Rescinded and Demand for Payment 129
Extension of Debt Payment Agreement 131
General Subordination 141
Information Request on Disputed Charges 153
Notice of Disputed Account 200
Notice of Unpaid Invoice 209
Notice to Creditor to Pay Specific Accounts 214
Notice to Reissue Cheque 222
Notice to Stop Credit Charge 225
Past Due Reminder 231
Payment Inquiry 232
Payment on Specific Accounts 233
Payment on Written Instrument 234
Payments to a Creditor 235
Presentment by Mail 242
Receipt of Note for Collection 257
Receipt on Account for Partial Payment 259
Request for Bank Credit Reference 265
Request for Credit Interchange 266
Request for Information on Overdue Account 267
Request for Prepayment 268
Request for Reference 269
Request to Reduce Balance 272
Return of Claim as Noncollectible 277
Sample Letter Requesting an Out-of-Court Settlement 282

Canadian Legal Forms and Agreements

Sample Letter Requesting Installment Payments 283
Second Notice of Overdue Account 286
Settlement of Disputed Account 288
Settlement Offer on Disputed Account 289
Transmittal for Collection 306
Waiver of Liability 314

V. Buying & Selling

Authorization to Return Goods 52
Bill of Sale 55
Confirmation of Verbal Agreement 71
Confirmation of Verbal Order 72
Defective Good Notice 85
Demand for Delivery 87
Exceptions to Purchase Order 125
Exclusive Right to Sell 126
Invitation to Quote Price of Goods 156
Notice of C.O.D. Terms 190
Notice of Cash-Only Terms 191
Notice of Corrected Account 194
Notice of Results of Public Sale 206
Notice of Wrongful Refusal to Accept Delivery 211
Notice to Cancel Back-Ordered Goods 212
Notice to Cancel Delayed Goods 213
Notice to Purchaser of Breach of Option 219
Notice to Reclaim Goods 220
Notice to Stop Goods in Transit 226
Partial Shipment Request 230
Product Defect Claim 244
Product Defect Notice 245
Proposal to Buy a Business 249
Purchase Requirement Agreement 250
Receipt on Account for Goods to be Delivered 258
Sale on Approval Acknowledgement 279
Schedule of Assets for Sale or Loan 285
Warranty Bill of Sale 319
Withheld Delivery Notice 320

VI. Leases & Tenancies

Agreement to Lease 22
Amendment to Lease 26

Assignment of Lease 42
Commercial Lease 65
Demand for Rent 92
Extension of Lease 132
Final Notice Before Legal Action 133
Guaranty of Rents 147
Landlord's and Tenant's Mutual Release 157
Landlord's Notice to Terminate Tenancy 158
Landlord's Notice to Vacate 159
Lease Termination Agreement 162
Notice of Change in Rent 192
Notice of Intent to Repossess Due to Default 203
Notice of Rent Arrears 205
Notice to Exercise Lease Option 216
Notice to Landlord to Make Repairs 217
Notice to Remedy Default by Tenant 223
Notice to Tenant to Make Repairs 227
Personal Property Rental Agreement 238
Release of Breach of Lease by Tenant 261
Residential Rental Application 273
Sublease 295
Tenant's Notice to Exercise Purchase Option 300
Tenant's Notice to Terminate Tenancy 301

VII. Transfers & Assignments

Assignment by Endorsing on Lease 33
Assignment of Accounts Receivable with Non-Recourse 34
Assignment of Accounts Receivable with Recourse 35
Assignment of Assets 36
Assignment of Bank Account 37
Assignment of Contract 38
Assignment of Damage Claim 39
Assignment of Income 40
Assignment of Insurance Policy 41
Assignment of Money Due 44
Assignment of Option 45
Consent to Assignment 75
Consent to Partial Assignment 76
General Assignment 139
Notice of Assignment 187
Notice of Assignment to Obligor 188
Notice of Debt Assignment 195

Purchaser's Assignment of Option 251
Renewal of Notice of Assignment of Accounts 263
Samples and Documents Receipt..284

VIII. Personal & Family
Accident Claim Notice 4
Address Change Notice...11
Authorization to Release Medical Information 51
Change of Beneficiary...59
Child Guardianship Consent Form 62
Cohabitation Agreement..63
Declaration of Trust..84
Insurance Claim Notice..155
Last Will and Testament...160
Lost Credit Card Notice 168
Mailing List Name Removal Request 169
Product Warranty Claim 246
Statement of Wishes..293
Trip Permission...307

IX. Business
Accident Report..5
Acknowledged Receipt of Goods 6
Acknowledgement of Modified Terms 7
Agreement on Proprietary Rights..13
Agreement Reminder 15
Certificate of Corporate Resolution...58
Letter of Commendation...164
List of Shareholders 167
Minutes of Annual Meeting of Stockholders 170
Minutes of Combined Meeting of Stockholders and Directors 172
Minutes of Directors' Meeting 174
Minutes of First Meeting of Shareholders 175
Minutes of Special Meeting of Stockholders 177
Notice of Annual Shareholders' Meeting 186
Notice of Waiver of Annual Meeting By All Shareholders 210
Notice to Directors of Special Meeting 215
Notice to Officer of Removal From Board 218
Notice to Shareholders of Annual Meeting..224
Option to Purchase Stock 229
Privacy Release...243
Stock Subscription..294
Waiver of Notice of Annual Meeting by Individual Shareholder..315

Waiver of Notice of Directors' Meeting 316
Waiver of Notice of Organization Meeting of Incorporators and Directors.........................317
Waiver of Notice—Combined Meeting..318
Written Unanimous Consent in Lieu of Meeting 321

X. Other Legal Forms

Authorization to Release Confidential Information 46
Bad Cheque Notice 53
Breach of Contract Notice 56
Cheque Stop-Payment 61
Demand for Contribution 86
Direct Deposit Authorization 98
Dishonored Cheque Placed for Bank Collection 100
Exercise of Option 128
Grant of Right to Use Name 142
Mutual Releases 180
Notice of Election to Cancel...201
Notice of Forfeiture...202
Option to Purchase 228
Release-Individual 262
Specific Release..292
Unsolicited Idea Acknowledgement 308
Waiver and Assumption of Risk 313

ABSENCE REQUEST

Employee: Date:

Department:

Date(s) Requested: From   to

Hours Requested: From   to

           With Pay (　)   Without Pay (　)   Make-up (　)

Reason for Absence:

                        Approved (　)   Not Approved (　)

Supervisor Comments:

_____   _____
Employee   Date

_____   _____
Supervisor   Date

ACCEPTANCE OF CLAIM

Date:

To:

Receipt is acknowledged of your claim against

for $. Your claim is accepted for collection under the following terms and conditions:

Our experience or contacts with the debtor are shown by check marks preceding the appropriate statements:

_____1. Personal demand is being made upon the debtor. A further report will be made to you in   days.

_____2. The debtor is slow in paying, but we believe that we can collect your claim without suit.

_____3. The debtor must be sued. If you desire suit to be filed, please send duplicate invoices, statements of account, and the enclosed affidavit, properly executed, together with your cheque for $ for advance court costs and suit fee. In the meantime, we shall try to effect an amicable settlement.

_____4. The debtor generally remits payment to the creditor immediately upon our demand. Kindly advise us of direct remittances.

_____5. The debtor is in bankruptcy. Please execute the enclosed proof of claim and power of attorney and return them to us at once.

_____6. We have had   claims against the debtor and have collected on   of them.

_____7. We now have   claims against the debtor and are collecting them by   .

_____8. This debtor disputes the claim. Please furnish additional information concerning the claim and send us all original correspondence, together with any original orders, written acknowledgements, or promises to pay.

_____9. This debtor is out of business. The debtor has no property that can be levied on, and the debtor is not earning sufficient wages for garnishment. However, we believe the debtor will pay when possible. We will try to persuade the debtor to pay and shall keep you advised unless you advise us to return the claim to you.

Very truly yours,

_____

ACCIDENT CLAIM NOTICE

Date:

To:

Dear

You are hereby notified of a claim against you for damages arising from the following accident or injury, to which I believe you and/or your agents are liable.

Description of Accident:

Date:

Time:

Location:

Please have your insurance representative or lawyer contact me as soon as possible.

Very truly yours,

_____
Name

_____
Address

_____
Telephone

ACCIDENT REPORT

Employee: Age: Sex:

Department: Supervisor:

Date of accident:

Nature of injuries:

Cause of accident:

If employee left work, time of leaving:

If employee returned to work, time of return:

Name and address of physician:

If hospitalized, name and address of hospital:

Actions undertaken to avoid similar incidents:

Comments:

_____   _____
Supervisor   Date

ACKNOWLEDGED RECEIPT OF GOODS

The undersigned hereby acknowledges timely receipt of the goods described on the attached invoice (or   ), on   , 20   .

The undersigned also acknowledges that said goods have been fully inspected, conform to order, and are in good condition without defect or damage.

Dated:

_____

ACKNOWLEDGEMENT OF MODIFIED TERMS

Date:

To:

Dear

Reference is made to the contract or order between us dated _____, 20____.

This letter will acknowledge that the contract or order is modified and superseded by the following agreed change in terms:

All other terms shall remain as stated.

Unless I/we immediately hear from you to the contrary, in writing, I/we shall assume said modification is mutually agreeable, and I/we shall proceed accordingly on the modified terms. Please acknowledge same below and return one copy for my/our file.

Very truly yours,

_____

The foregoing modification is acknowledged:

_____

ACKNOWLEDGEMENT OF TEMPORARY EMPLOYMENT

I, the undersigned, understand I am being employed by

_____ (Company) in a temporary position only and for such time as my services are required. I hereby acknowledge that this temporary employment does not entitle me to any special consideration for permanent employment. I further understand that my temporary employment may be terminated at any time without resort to any disciplinary procedures set forth for permanent employees. Furthermore, I understand that I am not eligible to participate in any fringe benefit programs or retirement program or any other programs available to permanent employees (unless required by law) and, in the event I am allowed to participate in said benefit or program, then my continued participation may be voluntarily withdrawn or terminated by the Company at any time and without reason.

_____
Employee

_____
Date

_____
Witness

ADDENDUM TO CONTRACT

Reference is made to a certain agreement by and between the undersigned parties, said agreement being dated _____, 20____. (Contract)

BE IT KNOWN, that for good consideration the parties make the following additions or changes a part of said contract as if contained therein:

All other terms and provisions of said contract shall remain in full force and effect.

Signed this ____ day of _____, 20____.

In the presence of:

_____ _____
Witness   First Party

_____ _____
Witness   Second Party

ADDENDUM TO EMPLOYMENT AGREEMENT

Reference is made to a certain agreement by and between _____ (Employee) and _____ (Company), said agreement being dated _____, 20____.

BE IT KNOWN, that for good consideration Employee and Company make the following additions or changes a part of said agreement as if contained therein:

All other terms and provisions of said agreement shall remain in full force and effect.

Signed this _____ day of _____, 20____.

_____
Company

_____
By

_____
Employee

ADDRESS CHANGE NOTICE

Date:

To:

Dear

    Please be advised that effective _____, 20____ , our address has been changed from:

_____

_____

to

_____

_____

    Our new telephone number is:

    Please make note of the above information and direct all correspondence to us at our new address. Thank you.

_____

AGREEMENT OF WAIVER OF RIGHT OF INHERITANCE

THIS AGREEMENT, made _____, 20____, by and between _____ (Husband) and _____ (Wife).

1. Recital. Husband and wife have each been previously married and have children by prior marriages. Husband desires that his children shall inherit his property, and Wife desires that her children shall inherit her property.

2. Waiver and Release. Accordingly, in consideration of our mutual promises and other valuable consideration, husband and wife waive any statutory or intestate right or interest that he or she has or may at any time have in any property now owned or subsequently acquired by the other. Each of the parties releases the other and his or her estate from any and all intestate interest, right, or distributive share that he or she may otherwise be entitled to on the death of the other, and waives the right to elect to take against any will or codicil made by the other that may be offered for or admitted to probate. The parties agree not to oppose but to permit the admission to probate of any will of the other, and to permit the other's estate to be administered by the person or persons legally entitled to do so as if they were not married.

_____ _____
Witness   Witness

IN WITNESS WHEREOF, we have subscribed our names on the day and year set forth.

_____ _____
Husband   Wife

AGREEMENT ON PROPRIETARY RIGHTS

Date:

Idea for:

    I represent to _____ (Company) that I now have suggestions, ideas or inventions, and may, in the future, have related suggestions, which I now request the Company consider for commercial exploitation. I understand that the Company cannot accept such suggestions in confidence; therefore, I agree to submit my suggestions to the Company under the following conditions:

    1. The Company's review of my suggestions is made only upon my request, and the Company accepts no responsibility for holding any submitted information in confidence.

    2. No obligation of any kind is assumed nor may be implied against the Company unless or until I have entered into a formal written contract with the Company pertaining to my submissions. In addition, any obligation shall be only such as is expressed in writing.

    3. Neither the Company nor any of its affiliates shall have any rights under any patents I now have nor may later obtain for my submissions covered by this letter, but, in consideration of their examining and considering same, I hereby release the Company from any liability in connection with my submissions or from liability because of their use of my submissions or of any portion thereof, except such liability as may accrue under valid patents now or hereafter issued. Subject to these conditions, I certify that I have made no prior disclosure to the Company or any of its affiliates regarding these submissions and that the entire disclosure now made by me to the Company is included in the attached papers listed below and submitted for retention by the Company. If, at any time, I correspond with or discuss my submissions with an officer, employee, agent or representative of the Company and, in the course of such correspondence or discussion, make any additional disclosures regarding such submissions, I shall, upon request, furnish the Company an illustration or a complete description, or both, of such additional disclosure, so that it can be made a part of the permanent record of the Company.

_____
Date

_____
Submitted by

_____
Address of Submitter

The following documents are attached and made a part of this agreement:

1.

2.

3.

4.

5.

6.

7.

8.

9.

10.

AGREEMENT REMINDER

Date:

To:

On _____, 20___, you promised to pay your overdue balance in _____ (weekly/monthly) payments of $_____ each.

We have not received your payment due _____, 20___. We assume this was simply an oversight, and you shall immediately remit your payment.

Please give this matter your immediate attention so we know you intend to comply with your agreed payment terms.

Very truly,

_____

AGREEMENT TO ACCEPT NIGHT WORK

A second shift is or may be required to meet our present or future needs. All new employees are hired with the understanding that they are able and willing to work nights.

Please answer the following:

	YES	NO
1. Do you have any physical disability that would prevent you from working nights?	_____	_____
2. Do you know of any personal reasons that would interfere with your working nights?	_____	_____
3. Are you willing to work nights?	_____	_____

I understand that any employment is conditioned upon my acceptance of a night assignment if required. Furthermore, I understand that I can be reassigned by the company to any plant or department. However, my requests for transfer will be considered only after I have successfully completed the requisite period of active employment with the company.

_____
Signed

_____
Date

_____
Witness

In case of emergency notify:

Name: _____ Phone: _____

Address: _____ Relationship: _____

Name: _____ Phone: _____

Address: _____ Relationship: _____

AGREEMENT TO ASSUME DEBT

FOR GOOD CONSIDERATION, and in consideration of _____ (Creditor) assenting to allow the transfer of certain assets from _____ (Customer) to the undersigned, the following is hereby acknowledged and agreed by the parties:

1. The undersigned acknowledges that Customer presently owes Creditor the sum of $ _____ (debt).

2. The undersigned unconditionally and irrevocably agrees to assume and pay said debt, and otherwise guarantees to Creditor the payment of same and to indemnify and hold harmless Creditor from any loss thereto.

3. Said debt shall be punctually due and payable in the manner following: (Describe terms)

4. Nothing herein shall constitute a release or discharge of the obligations of Customer to Creditor for the payment of said debt, provided that so long as the undersigned shall promptly pay the debt in the manner above described, Creditor shall forebear in commencing any action against Customer. In the event of any default, Creditor shall have full rights, jointly and severally, against both Customer and/or undersigned for any balance then owing.

5. This agreement shall be binding upon and inure to the benefit of the parties, their successors, assigns and personal representatives.

Signed this _____ day of _____ , 20____ .

_____

Assented to:

_____
Creditor

_____
Customer

AGREEMENT TO COMPROMISE DEBT

FOR VALUE RECEIVED, the undersigned, being a creditor of _____ (Customer), hereby agrees to compromise and reduce the indebtedness due the undersigned upon the following terms and conditions:

1. The customer and the undersigned acknowledge that the present debt due the customer from the undersigned is $_____.

2. The parties agree that the undersigned shall accept $_____ as full and total payment on said debt and in complete discharge and satisfaction of all monies due, provided said sum herein is punctually paid as follows:

3. Should customer fail to punctually pay the agreed amount, the undersigned shall have full rights to prosecute its claim for the total debt due under Paragraph 1 above, less payments made.

4. Upon default, the customer agrees to pay all reasonable lawyer's fees and costs of collection.

5. This agreement shall be binding upon and inure to the benefit of the parties, their successors, assigns and personal representatives.

Signed this _____ day of _____, 20____.

_____
Creditor

_____
Company

AGREEMENT TO EXTEND DEBT PAYMENT

FOR VALUE RECEIVED, the undersigned, _____ (Creditor) and _____ (Customer), hereby acknowledge and agree to the following:

1. Customer presently owes the Creditor the sum of $_____, said amount being presently due and payable.

2. In consideration of Creditor's forbearance, the Customer agrees to pay said debt on extended terms, together with interest on the unpaid balance of _____ % per annum, payable in the following manner:

3. In the event the Customer shall fail to make any payment on the due date, Creditor shall have full rights to proceed for the collection of the entire balance then remaining which shall be immediately due and payable.

4. In the event of default, Customer agrees to pay all reasonable lawyer's fees and costs necessary for the collection hereof.

5. At the election of Creditor, Customer agrees to execute note(s) evidencing the then remaining balance due on terms otherwise consistent with this agreement.

6. During the pendency of this agreement, Creditor shall ship to Customer only on a C.O.D. basis. Earned discounts or other trade concessions, if applicable, shall be applied to the debt payments in inverse order of maturity.

7. This agreement shall be binding upon and inure to the benefit of the parties, their successors and assigns.

Signed this _____ day of _____, 20___.

_____
Creditor

_____
Customer

AGREEMENT TO EXTEND PERFORMANCE DATE

BE IT KNOWN, for good consideration,

of _____ (First Party), and

_____ of

_____ (Second Party),

in and to a certain agreement described as:

dated _____, 20____, (Agreement) do hereby acknowledge and agree that:

1. Said Agreement provides that full performance of said Agreement shall be completed on or before _____, 20____.

2. That the parties acknowledge that said Agreement cannot be performed and completed on said date and that the parties hereupon desire to extend the performance date, as if said extended date were the original date of performance.

3. That the parties hereby mutually agree that the date for performance be continued and extended to _____, 20____, time being of the essence.

4. There is no other change in terms or further extension allowed.

This agreement shall be binding upon and inure to the benefit of the parties, their successors and assigns.

Signed this _____ day of _____, 20____.

In the presence of:

_____   _____
Witness   First Party

_____   _____
Witness   Second Party

AGREEMENT TO EXTEND PERIOD OF OPTION

In consideration of the additional sum of
_____ Dollars ($_____) paid to _____,
(hereinafter "Seller"), by _____, (hereinafter "Purchaser"), the
period of that certain option from Seller to Purchaser dated _____, 20___,
is hereby extended to _____ o'clock ___.m., _____, 20___.

The extension shall apply to all terms, provisions, and conditions of the option and shall be binding and inure to the Purchaser, his heirs, representatives, and assigns.

IN WITNESS WHEREOF, the parties have executed this instrument on _____,
20___.

Witnessed:

_____   _____
Witness   Seller

_____   _____
Witness   Purchaser

AGREEMENT TO LEASE

This agreement, made this   day of   , 20   , between   (hereinafter "Lessor") and   (hereinafter "Lessee").

Lessor does hereby agree to grant, demise and let, and Lessee does hereby agree to take   , with appurtenances, from the   day of   , 20   to the   day of   , 20   , at the rent or sum of   Dollars ($), to be paid as follows:

It is further agreed by and between the parties that the Lessor shall:

It is further agreed by and between the parties that the Lessee shall:

It is further agreed that the lease herein provided for shall be executed by the parties hereto on the   day of   , 20   .

It is further agreed that in the event that the lease herein provided for shall be executed, then and in such case the Lessor shall give, and the Lessee shall take, possession of said premises on the   day of   , 20   , and the rent to be reserved in the said agreement herein provided for shall commence and be payable from said last mentioned date.

It is further agreed that, in the event that either party hereto shall neglect, refuse or in any way fail to execute the lease herein provided for, at said time and place, then the party in default shall pay to the other party the sum of   Dollars ($) as liquidated damages and not as a penalty.

It is further agreed that the lease shall contain the following further provisions:

It is further agreed that these presents shall operate only as an agreement to lease, and not as a lease.

IN WITNESS WHEREOF, the parties hereto sign their names.

Witnessed:

_____   _____
Witness   Lessor

_____   _____
Witness   Lessee

AGREEMENT TO PURCHASE STOCK

For and in consideration of _____ Dollars ($ _____), _____ hereby agrees to sell, assign, transfer, and set over to _____ , his or her executors, representatives, and assigns, with full power to transfer the same on the books of the corporation, _____ shares of the _____ stock of _____ , a corporation incorporated under the laws of the Province of _____ , and having its principal place of business at _____ . The stock is represented by the following certificates:

Seller warrants that the stock now stands in his or her name on the books of the corporation and that all assessments to date are paid upon said shares.

_____ agrees to purchase said shares for the consideration set forth above.

IN WITNESS WHEREOF, the parties have executed this stock purchase agreement on _____ , 20 ___ .

_____ _____
Buyer   Seller

AGREEMENT TO SELL PERSONAL PROPERTY

Purchase and Sales Agreement made by and between _____ of _____ (Seller) and _____ of _____ (Buyer).

Whereas, for good consideration the parties mutually agree that:

1. Seller agrees to sell, and Buyer agrees to buy, the following described property:

2. Buyer agrees to pay to Seller, and Seller agrees to accept as total purchase price, the sum of $ _____ , payable as follows:

    $ _____ deposit herewith paid

    $ _____ balance payable on delivery by cash, bank or certified cheque

3. Seller warrants it has good and legal title to said property, full authority to sell said property, and that said property shall be sold by warranty bill of sale free and clear of all liens, encumbrances, liabilities and adverse claims of every nature and description whatsoever.

4. Said property is sold in "as is" condition, Seller disclaiming any warranty of merchantability, fitness or working order or condition of the property except that it shall be sold in its present condition, reasonable wear and tear excepted.

5. The parties agree to transfer title on _____ , 20 _____ at the address of the Seller.

6. This agreement shall be binding upon and inure to the benefit of the parties, their successors, assigns and personal representatives.

Signed this _____ day of _____ , 20 _____ .

_____   _____
Witness   Seller

_____   _____
Witness   Buyer

AMENDMENT TO LEASE

BE IT KNOWN, that for good consideration of _____ (Landlord), and _____ of _____ (Tenant), under a certain lease agreement between them for premises known as _____, dated _____, 20___ (Lease), hereby agree to modify and amend said Lease as to the following terms:

All other Lease terms shall remain in force as contained in the original Lease, which provisions are incorporated herein by reference.

This Lease Amendment shall become a part of the original Lease and shall be binding upon and inure to the benefit of the parties, their successors, assigns and personal representatives.

Signed under seal this _____ day of _____, 20___.

In the presence of:

_____   _____
Witness   Landlord

_____   _____
Witness   Tenant

ANALYSIS OF CASH AVAILABLE FOR DEBT REPAYMENT

Month of _____

Food .... $_____

Rent/Mortgage .... $_____

Telephone .... $_____

Water & Power .... $_____

Electric & Gas.. $_____

Insurance

    Health .... $_____

    Auto .... $_____

    Homeowners .... $_____

    Life .... $_____

Child Care .... $_____

Car Payments .... $_____

Gasoline/Travel .... $_____

Medical .... $_____

Other .... $_____

.... $_____

Total Necessary Expenses........................ $_____

After Tax Income .... $_____

Less: Necessary Expense .... $_____

**Amount Available for Payments
    or (Amount Short)** .... $_____

APPLICANT ACKNOWLEDGEMENT

Date:

To:

Thank you for responding to our advertisement for the position of

.

Your qualifications, as communicated in your letter and resume, appear to meet the minimum requirements for the position. As scheduling permits, we would like to arrange for an interview at our offices located at

.

Please call   at to make an appointment for your interview.

Thank you for your interest in the above position.

Sincerely,

_____

Personnel Manager

APPLICANT INTERVIEW CONFIRMATION

Date:

To:

This will confirm your appointment for an interview for the position of _____. The interview will be at our offices located at _____ at _____ m. You can expect the interview to take approximately _____ hours.

You will first meet with _____, the _____. You are scheduled to meet later with _____.

After the interview, we will contact you regarding our decision.

Once again, thank you for your interest in our firm. We look forward to seeing you on the above date.

Sincerely,

_____
Personnel Manager

APPLICANT NOTIFICATION

Date:

To:

Dear   :

      I am in receipt of your letter and resume in response to our ad for the   position. Thank you for your interest in our firm.

      We have been unsuccessful in our attempts to reach you by phone.

      I am available to discuss our job opening with you if you remain interested. Please contact me at your earliest convenience at this telephone number:

      I look forward to hearing from you.

                                                    Sincerely,

_____

APPLICANT REFERRAL PROGRAM

To:

Date:

From:

Thank you for your recent referral of

for the position of   .

The status of this candidate is:

_____ No longer interested in employment.

_____ Job was offered and declined.

_____ Job offer is pending.

_____ Currently being interviewed.

_____ Resume on file; no current openings.

_____ Not qualified.

Thank you for your support and participation in the employee referral program. If any further action is taken regarding this candidate, we will notify you.

_____
Personnel Manager

APPLICANT WAIVER

(All job applicants must sign and submit with application form)

I hereby certify that the information hereunder is correct to the best of my knowledge and understand that falsification of this information is grounds for refusal to hire or, if hired, dismissal.

I hereby authorize any of the persons or organizations listed in my application to give all information concerning my previous employment, education, or any other information they might have, personal or otherwise, with regard to any of the subjects covered by this application, and release all such parties from all liability that may result from furnishing such information to you. I authorize you to request and receive such information.

In consideration for my employment and my being considered for employment by your company, I agree to adhere to the rules and regulations of the company and hereby acknowledge that these rules and regulations may be changed by your company at any time, at the company's sole option and without any prior notice. In addition, I acknowledge that my employment may be terminated, and any offer of employment, if such is made, may be withdrawn, with or without prior notice, at any time, at the option of either the company or myself.

I understand that no representative of the company has any authority to enter into any agreement for employment for any specified period of time, or to assure or make some other personnel move, either prior to commencement of employment or after I have become employed, or to assure any benefits or terms and conditions of employment, or to make any agreement, that is contrary to the foregoing.

I hereby acknowledge that I have been advised that this application will remain active for no more than 90 days from the date it was signed.

Applicant: _____   Date: _____

Company
Representative: _____   Date: _____

ASSIGNMENT BY ENDORSING ON LEASE

BE IT KNOWN, that for good and valuable consideration received, the undersigned Lessee hereby assigns all the Lessee's right, title, and interest in and to the within lease from and after _____, 20___, to _____, 20___, to _____, said premises to be used and occupied for _____ and no other purpose. We further agree that this assignment shall not release or relieve the undersigned, as original Lessee, from any liability under covenants of the lease.

Date: _____   _____

ASSIGNMENT OF ACCOUNTS RECEIVABLE
WITH NON-RECOURSE

FOR VALUE RECEIVED, the undersigned hereby assigns and transfers to _____ all rights, title and interest in and to the account(s) receivable described as follows:

The undersigned warrants that the said account(s) are just and due, and the undersigned has not received payment for same or any part thereof and has no knowledge of any dispute thereon, provided however, that said account(s) are sold without recourse to the undersigned in the event of non-payment.

The undersigned further warrants that it has full title to said receivables, full authority to sell and transfer same, and that said receivables are sold free and clear of all liens, encumbrances or any known claims against said account(s).

This agreement shall be binding upon and inure to the benefit of the parties, their successors, assigns, and personal representatives.

Signed this _____ day of _____, 20____.

_____

Signed in the presence of:

_____
Witness

ASSIGNMENT OF ACCOUNTS RECEIVABLE
WITH RECOURSE

FOR VALUE RECEIVED, the undersigned hereby assigns and transfers to   all right, title and interest in and to the account(s) receivable described as follows:

The undersigned warrants that said account(s) are just and due and the undersigned has not received payment for same or any part thereof.

It is further provided that if any said account does not make full payment within   days, said account(s) will be re-purchased by the undersigned and the undersigned shall re-purchase same for the balance then owing on said account(s), the undersigned thereby guaranteeing collection of said receivables.

The undersigned further warrants that it has full title to said receivables, full authority to sell and transfer same, and that said receivables are sold free and clear of all liens, encumbrances or any known claims against said account(s).

This agreement shall be binding upon and inure to the benefit of the parties, their successors, assigns, and personal representatives.

Signed this   day of   , 20   .

_____

Signed in the presence of:

_____
Witness

ASSIGNMENT OF ASSETS
TO

_____

BE IT KNOWN, for value received, the undersigned _____ of _____ hereby unconditionally and irrevocably assigns and transfers unto _____ of _____ all right, title and interest in and to the following:

The undersigned fully warrants that it has full rights and authority to enter into this assignment and that the rights and benefits assigned hereunder are free and clear of any lien, encumbrance, adverse claim or interest by any third party.

This assignment shall be binding upon and inure to the benefit of the parties, and their successors and assigns.

Signed this _____ day of _____, 20___.

_____   _____
Witness   Assignor

_____   _____
Witness   Assignee

ASSIGNMENT OF BANK ACCOUNT

BE IT KNOWN, that for consideration the undersigned, _____,
hereby sells, assigns, transfers and irrevocably sets over to _____,
_____ Dollars ($_____) of the sums on deposit in
my name (Savings Account No. _____) in the
_____ Bank, located at _____, and further authorizes said
bank to pay over to _____, Assignee,
said sum out of the money on deposit in said bank account in the undersigned's name.

This assignment shall constitute notice to the _____
Bank of this assignment and direct authorization to such bank to act on this assignment.

IN WITNESS WHEREOF, the undersigned executed this assignment on
_____, 20_____.

Witnessed:

_____   _____
Witness   Seller

ASSIGNMENT OF CONTRACT

FOR VALUE RECEIVED, the undersigned Assignor hereby assigns, transfers and sets over to _____ (Assignee) all rights, title and interest held by the Assignor in and to the following described contract:

The Assignor warrants and represents that said contract is in full force and effect and is fully assignable.

The Assignee hereby assumes and agrees to perform all the remaining and executory obligations of the Assignor under the contract and agrees to indemnify and hold the Assignor harmless from any claim or demand resulting from non-performance by the Assignee.

The Assignee shall be entitled to all monies remaining to be paid under the contract, which rights are also assigned hereunder.

The Assignor warrants that the contract is without modification and remains on the terms contained.

The Assignor further warrants that it has full right and authority to transfer said contract and that the contract rights herein transferred are free of lien, encumbrance or adverse claim.

This assignment shall be binding upon and inure to the benefit of the parties, their successors and assigns.

Signed this _____ day of _____, 20___.

_____   _____
Witness   Assignor

_____   _____
Witness   Assignee

ASSIGNMENT OF DAMAGE CLAIM

BE IT KNOWN, for value received, the undersigned hereby unconditionally and irrevocably assigns and transfers unto
(Assignee) and its successors, assigns and personal representatives, any and all claims, demands, and cause or causes of action of any kind whatsoever which the undersigned has or may have against   arising from the following:

The Assignee may in its own name, at its own expense, and for its own benefit prosecute said claim and collect, settle, compromise and grant releases on said claim as it in its sole discretion deems advisable, provided the undersigned shall reasonably assist and cooperate in the prosecution of said claim to the extent required or requested. Assignee shall be entitled to all judgments, awards and payments thereon.

The undersigned warrants it has full right and authority to assign this claim and that said claim is free and clear of any lien, encumbrance or other adverse interest. Assignor disclaims any representation as to the merits or collectibility of such claim.

This assignment shall be binding upon and inure to the benefit of the parties, their successors, assigns and personal representatives.

Signed this   day of   , 20   .

In the presence of:

_____   _____
Witness   Assignor

ASSIGNMENT OF INCOME

FOR VALUE RECEIVED, the undersigned hereby assigns and transfers to _____ (Creditor) all rights to proceeds, income, rentals, fees, profits, or monies due the undersigned from _____, under a certain obligation described as:

Said income shall be applied to a certain debt presently due Creditor in the amount of $ _____. Any surplus above said amount shall be remitted to the undersigned. In the event said income shall not fully discharge the amount due Creditor within _____ days, Creditor shall have full recourse against undersigned on any deficiency then due.

Signed this _____ day of _____, 20 ___.

_____

ASSIGNMENT OF INSURANCE POLICY

BE IT KNOWN, for value received, the undersigned _____ of _____ hereby irrevocably transfers and assigns to _____ all legal and beneficial right, title and interest in and to the within policy of insurance standing in my name and known as Policy No. _____ issued by the _____ Insurance Company. I also assign all cash values, proceeds and benefits thereto arising, subject to the conditions of said policy and the requirement of the issuing underwriter.

The undersigned warrants that it has full authority to transfer said policy and shall execute all further documents as may be required by the underwriter.

This assignment shall be binding upon and inure to the benefit of the parties, their successors, assigns and personal representatives.

Signed this _____ day of _____, 20____.

In the presence of:

_____   _____
Witness   Name

                                    _____
                                    Address

                                    _____

ASSIGNMENT OF LEASE

AGREEMENT by and between   (Tenant), and   (Assignee), and   (Landlord).

For value received, it is agreed by and between the parties that:

1. Tenant hereby agrees to assign, transfer and deliver to Assignee all of Tenant's remaining rights in and to a certain lease between Tenant and Landlord for premises known as:

,

under lease dated   , 20   .

2. Assignee agrees to accept said Lease, pay all rents and punctually perform all of Tenant's remaining obligations under said Lease accruing after the date of delivery of possession to the Assignee as contained herein. Assignee further agrees to indemnify and save harmless the Tenant from any breach of Assignee's obligations hereunder.

3. The parties acknowledge that Tenant shall deliver possession of the leased premises to Assignee on   , 20   , (effective date); time being of the essence. All rights and other charges accrued under the Lease prior to said date shall be fully paid by Tenant, and thereafter by the Assignee.

4. Landlord hereby assents to the assignment of lease, provided that:

    a) Assent to the assignment shall not discharge Tenant of its obligations to pay rent under the Lease in the event of breach by Assignee.

    b) In the event of breach by Assignee, Landlord shall provide Tenant with written notice of same, and Tenant shall have full rights to recover possession of the leased premises (in the name of Landlord, if necessary) and retain all rights for the duration of said Lease provided it shall pay all accrued rents and cure any other default.

5. The parties acknowledge the lease to be in good standing and in full force and effect without modification.

6. This agreement shall be binding upon and inure to the benefit of the parties, their successors, assigns and personal representatives.

      Signed this _____ day of _____, 20___.

In the presence of:

_____   _____
Witness   Tenant

_____   _____
Witness   Assignee

_____   _____
Witness   Landlord

ASSIGNMENT OF MONEY DUE

BE IT KNOWN, that for good and valuable consideration received, the undersigned, _____, assigns, transfers, and sets over to _____, Assignee, all money now due and payable to me and to become due and payable to the undersigned under a certain contract dated _____, 20____, between the undersigned and _____, Obligor, the subject matter of which is:

.

The undersigned hereby warrants that there has been no breach of the aforementioned contract by any party, and that the undersigned is in full compliance with all the terms and conditions of said contract, and has not assigned or encumbered all or any rights under said contract.

The undersigned authorizes and directs _____, Obligor, to deliver any and all cheques, drafts, or payments to be issued pursuant to such contract to Assignee, and further authorizes Assignee to receive such cheques, drafts, or payments from Obligor, and to endorse my name on them and to collect any and all funds due or to become due pursuant thereto.

IN WITNESS WHEREOF, the undersigned executed this assignment on _____, 20____.

_____   _____
Witness   Assignor

ASSIGNMENT OF OPTION

In consideration of the payment to the undersigned of   Dollars ($), receipt of which is hereby acknowledged, the undersigned hereby sells, transfers, assigns, and sets over the foregoing option unto   all my rights, title and interest in and to the following:

By accepting this assignment the Assignee undertakes and agrees to exercise the option pursuant to its terms.

Date:

_____   _____
Witness   Signature of Assignor

AUTHORIZATION TO RELEASE CONFIDENTIAL INFORMATION

Date:

To:

Dear

You are hereby authorized and requested to mail or deliver to:

_____
Name

_____
Address

_____

either original or copies of the below described documents or confidential information that you may have in your possession:

You may bill me for any costs associated with your compliance with this request, and I thank you for your cooperation.

Very truly yours,

_____
Name

_____
Address

_____

AUTHORIZATION TO RELEASE CREDIT INFORMATION

Date:

To:

    Please be advised I have a credit account with your firm and hereby request that a report of my credit history with you be forwarded to the below listed credit reporting agencies. You may consider this letter as my authorization to release this information.

    Thank you for your cooperation.

_____
Signature

_____
Social Insurance Number

_____
Address

_____

_____
Signature of Joint Applicant (if any)

_____
Name of Account

_____
Account Number

Credit Reporting Agencies/Company

_____   _____
Agency/Company   Agency/Company

_____   _____
Address   Address

_____   _____

_____   _____
ATTN: ATTN:

AUTHORIZATION TO RELEASE EMPLOYMENT INFORMATION

Date:

To:

    The undersigned _____ (Employee) authorizes the release of the below checked employment information to:

    _____ The following party:

    _____ Any third party:

Those terms for which information may be released include: (Check)

    _____ Salary
    _____ Position and department
    _____ Dates of employment
    _____ Part-time/Full-time hours worked
    _____ Garnishes or wage attachments, if any
    _____ Reason for separation
    _____ Medical/accident/illness reports
    _____ Work performance rating
    _____ Other:

Thank you for your cooperation.

_____   _____
Employee Signature   Social Insurance Number

_____   _____
Address   Position or Title

_____   _____
Date of Employment   Position or Department

AUTHORIZATION TO RELEASE FINANCIAL STATEMENTS

Date:

To:

    We have found that as our customers' businesses change, so do their credit needs. Consequently, we work closely with them and periodically review their financial situations so we can establish new credit terms.

    The most convenient way to accomplish this for many of our customers is to furnish us with updated financial information, and to authorize their accountant to forward us copies of their financial statements each year.

    If you would like to participate in this annual review program, please sign below. This authorizes your accountant to send us your financial statements annually. Upon our review we shall inform you concerning recommended changes in your credit terms.

    You may, of course, terminate this authorization at any time. All information received shall be held in strict confidence.

Very truly,

\
To:
_____ (Accounting Firm)

_____ (Address)

    You are authorized and directed to send copies of our annual financial statements to the above until further notice.

_____
Customer

AUTHORIZATION TO RELEASE INFORMATION

From:

To:

I have applied for a position with   .

I have been requested to provide information for their use in reviewing my background and qualifications. Therefore, I hereby authorize the investigation of my past and present work, character, education, military and employment qualifications.

The release in any manner of all information by you is hereby authorized whether such information is of record or not, and I do hereby release all persons, agencies, firms, companies, etc., from any damages resulting from providing such information.

This authorization is valid for _____ days from date below. Please keep this copy of my release request for your files. Thank you.

Signature_____   Date_____

Witness_____   Date_____

AUTHORIZATION TO RELEASE MEDICAL INFORMATION

Date:

To:

Dear

I hereby authorize and request that you release and deliver to:

all my medical records, charts, files, prognoses, reports, x-rays, laboratory reports, clinical records, and such other information relative to my medical condition or my treatment at any time provided to me and all to the extent said information is available and within your possession. You may bill me for any costs. You are further requested not to disclose any information concerning my past or present medical condition to any other person without my express written permission.

Thank you for your cooperation.

In the presence of:

_____   _____
Witness   Releasor

_____   _____
Name of Witness   Name of Releasor

_____   _____
Address of Witness   Address of Releasor

AUTHORIZATION TO RETURN GOODS

Date:

To:

Please allow this letter to acknowledge that we shall accept certain return goods for credit. The terms for return are:

1. The aggregate cost value of the goods subject to return shall not exceed $.

2. We shall deduct   % of the cost price as handling charges to process the return goods, crediting your account.

3. All return goods shall be in re-saleable condition and represent goods we either currently stock or can return to our supplier for credit. We reserve the right to reject non-conforming goods.

4. Return goods must be invoiced and are subject to inspection and return approval before shipment to us.

5. If goods are shipped via common carrier, you shall be responsible for all freight costs and risk of loss in transit. Goods shall not be considered accepted for return until we have received, inspected and approved said goods at our place of business.

6. Our agreement to accept returns for credit is expressly conditional upon your agreement to pay any remaining balance due on the following terms:

You understand this return privilege is extended only to resolve your account balance and is not necessarily standing policy. Thank you for your cooperation in this matter.

Very truly yours,

_____

BAD CHEQUE NOTICE

Date:

To:

Dear

    Payment on your Cheque No. _____ in the amount of $ _____, tendered to us on _____, 20___, has been dishonored by your bank. We have verified with your bank that there are still insufficient funds to pay the cheque.

    Accordingly, we request that you replace this cheque with a cash (or certified cheque) payment.

    Unless we receive good funds for said amount within _____ days, we shall immediately commence appropriate legal action to protect our interests. Upon receipt of replacement funds we shall return to you the dishonored cheque.

Face amount of cheque:	$_____
Service charge:	$_____
Total amount due:	$_____

Very truly yours,

_____

Registered Mail

BALLOON NOTE

FOR VALUE RECEIVED, the undersigned promise to pay to the order of _____ the sum of _____ Dollars ($ _____), with annual interest of _____ % on any unpaid balance.

This note shall be paid in _____ consecutive and equal installments of $ _____ each with a first payment one _____ from date hereof, and the same amount on the same day of each _____ thereafter, provided the entire principal balance and any accrued but unpaid interest shall be fully paid on or before _____, 20 _____ . This note may be prepaid without penalty. All payments shall be first applied to interest and the balance to principal.

This note shall be due and payable upon demand of any holder hereof should the undersigned default in any payment beyond _____ days of its due date. All parties to this note waive presentment, demand and protest, and all notices thereto. In the event of default, the undersigned agree to pay all costs of collection and reasonable lawyer's fees. The undersigned shall be jointly and severally liable under this note.

Signed this _____ day of _____, 20 _____ .

Signed in the presence of:

_____   _____
Witness   Maker

_____   _____
Witness   Maker

BILL OF SALE

FOR VALUE RECEIVED, the undersigned _____ of _____ hereby sells and transfers unto _____ of _____ (Buyer), and its successors and assigns forever, the following described goods and chattels:

Seller warrants and represents that it has good title to said property, full authority to sell and transfer same, and that said goods and chattels are being sold free and clear of all liens, encumbrances, liabilities and adverse claims of every nature and description.

Seller further warrants that it shall fully defend, protect, indemnify and save harmless the Buyer and its lawful successors and assigns from any and all adverse claims that may be made by any party against said goods.

It is provided, however, that Seller disclaims any implied warranty of condition, merchantability or fitness for a particular purpose. Said goods are being sold in their present condition "as is" and "where is."

Signed this _____ day of _____, 20____.

In the presence of:

_____   _____
Witness   Seller's Signature

                                                                                  _____
                                                                                  Seller's Address

_____   _____
Witness   Buyer's Signature

                                                                                  _____
                                                                                  Buyer's Address

BREACH OF CONTRACT NOTICE

Date:

To:

Dear

    Reference is made to a certain agreement between us dated _____, 20____, which agreement provides that:

    PLEASE TAKE NOTICE that you are in breach of your obligations under said contract in the following particulars:

    You are further advised that we shall hold you responsible for all actual and consequential damages arising from your breach.

Very truly yours,

_____
Signature

_____
Name

_____
Address

CANCELLATION OF STOP-PAYMENT ORDER

Date:

To:

Dear

    On _____, 20___, we advised you to stop payment on the following cheque:

        Cheque No.:

        Dated:

        Amount:

        Maker:

        Payable to:

        Account No.:

    You may now honor and pay said cheque upon presentment since we cancel this previously issued stop-payment order.

_____
Account

_____
Account No.

By:_____

CERTIFICATE OF CORPORATE RESOLUTION

_____

I, _____, Secretary of _____, (Corporation) do hereby certify that at a duly constituted meeting of the Stockholders and Directors of the Corporation held at the office of the Corporation on _____, 20___, it was upon motion duly made and seconded, that it be VOTED:

It was upon further motion made and seconded that it be further VOTED: That _____ in the capacity as _____ of the Corporation is empowered, authorized and directed to execute, deliver and accept any and all documents and undertake all acts reasonably required or incidental to accomplish the foregoing vote, all on such terms and conditions as he in his discretion deems to be in the best interests of the Corporation.

I further certify that the foregoing votes are in full force this date without rescission, modification or amendment.

Signed this _____ day of _____, 20___.

A TRUE RECORD

ATTEST

_____
Secretary/Clerk

(Corporate Seal)

CHANGE OF BENEFICIARY

Date:

To:

Notice is hereby given to you to change the beneficiary on Policy No.   , of   . The policy was issued by   (hereinafter "Company"). Subject to the provisions attached and marked as Exhibit A, the beneficiary is to be changed from   of   to   of   .

This request for change of beneficiary shall take effect as of the day it is signed, accepted, and recorded at the home office of the Company. Any previous selection of a beneficiary is hereby revoked.

_____

CHANGE WORK ORDER

Hirer:

Contractor:

Contract Date:

    1. The Hirer authorizes and the Contractor agrees to make the following work changes to the above dated contract:

    2. The agreed additional charge for the above change is
        Dollars ($).

Dated:

_____   _____
Hirer   Contractor

CHEQUE STOP-PAYMENT

Date:

To:

Dear

    Please be advised that you are hereby directed to place a stop-payment order and refuse payment against our account upon presentment of the following cheque:

        Name of Payee:

        Date of Cheque:

        Cheque Number:

        Amount:

This stop-payment order shall remain in effect until further written notice.

Please advise if this cheque has been previously paid, and the date of payment.

Thank you for your cooperation.

_____
Name of Account

_____
Account Number

By:_____

CHILD GUARDIANSHIP CONSENT FORM

The undersigned _____, of _____, Province of _____, hereby appoint _____, of _____, Province of _____, as the legal guardian of the person of our child(ren). Said guardian shall have the following powers:

Executed this _____ day of _____, 20___.

_____

_____

COHABITATION AGREEMENT

BE IT KNOWN, this agreement is made this   day of   ,
20   , by   and
who presently reside in the Province of   .

1. RELATIONSHIP: The parties wish to live together in a relationship similar to matrimony but do not wish to be bound by the statutory or common-law provisions relating to marriage.

2. DURATION OF RELATIONSHIP: It is agreed that we will live together for an indefinite period of time subject to the following terms:

3. PROPERTY: Any real or personal property acquired by us or either of us during the relationship shall be considered to be our separate property. All property listed on the pages attached is made a part of this agreement by this reference. The property now and hereinafter belongs to the party under whose name it is listed prior to the making of this agreement. All listed property is and shall continue to be the separate property of the person who now owns it. All property received by either of us by gift or inheritance during our relationship shall be the separate property of the one who receives it.

4. INCOME: All income of either of us and all our accumulations during the existence of our relationship shall be maintained in one fund. Our debts and expenses arising during the existence of our union shall be paid out of this fund. Each of us shall have an equal interest in this sum, and equal right to its management and control, and be equally entitled to the surplus remaining after payment of all debts and expenses.

5. TERMINATION: Our relationship may be terminated at the sole will and decision of either of us, expressed by a written notice given to the other.

6. MODIFICATION OF THIS AGREEMENT: This agreement may be modified by an agreement in writing by both parties, with the exception that no modifications may decrease the obligations that may be imposed regarding any children born of our union.

7. APPLICATION OF LAW: The validity of this agreement shall be determined solely under the laws of the Province of _____ as they may from time to time be changed.

8. NEITHER PARTY shall maintain any action or claim as against the other for support, alimony, compensation or for rights to any property existing prior to this date, or acquired during or subsequent to the date of termination.

9. THE PARTIES ENTER into this agreement of their own will and accord without reliance on any other inducement or promise.

10. EACH PARTY TO THIS AGREEMENT has had the opportunity to have this agreement reviewed by independent counsel.

Signed this _____ day of _____, 20___.

_____
First Party

_____
Second Party

COMMERCIAL LEASE

This lease is made between   , herein called Lessor (Landlord), and   , herein called Lessee (Tenant).

Lessee hereby offers to lease from Lessor the premises situated in the City of   , County of   , Province of   , described as   , upon the following TERMS and CONDITIONS:

1. TERM AND RENT. Lessor demises the above premises for a term of   years, commencing   , 20   , and terminating on   , 20   , or sooner as provided herein at the annual rental of   Dollars ($) payable in equal installments in advance on the first day of each month for that month's rental, during the term of this lease. All rental payments shall be made to Lessor, at the address specified above. Should the Tenant continue to occupy the Premises with the consent of the Landlord after the expiry of the term of the lease, Tenant shall be deemed to be leasing the premises on a month-to-month basis under the same terms as set forth in this lease.

2. USE. Lessee shall use and occupy the premises for   .
The premises shall be used for no other purpose. Lessor represents that the premises may lawfully be used for such purpose.

3. CARE AND MAINTENANCE OF PREMISES. Lessee acknowledges that the premises are in good order and repair, unless otherwise indicated herein. Lessee shall, at his own expense and at all times, maintain the premises in good and safe condition, including plate glass, electrical wiring, plumbing and heating installations and any other system or equipment upon the premises, and shall surrender the same at termination hereof, in as good condition as received, normal wear and tear excepted. Lessee shall be responsible for all repairs required, excepting the roof, exterior walls, structural foundations, and:

which shall be maintained by Lessor. Lessee shall also maintain in good condition such portions adjacent to the premises, such as sidewalks, driveways, lawns and shrubbery, which would otherwise be required to be maintained by Lessor.

4. ALTERATIONS. Lessee shall not, without first obtaining the written consent of Lessor, make any alterations, additions, or improvements, in, to or about the premises.

5. ORDINANCES AND STATUTES. Lessee shall comply with all statutes, ordinances and requirements of all municipal, provincial and federal authorities now in force, or which may hereafter be in force, pertaining to the premises, occasioned by or affecting the use thereof by Lessee.

6. ASSIGNMENT AND SUBLETTING. Lessee shall not assign this lease or sublet any portion of the premises without prior written consent of the Lessor, which shall not be unreasonably withheld. Any such assignment or subletting without consent shall be void and, at the option of the Lessor, may terminate this lease.

7. UTILITIES. All applications and connections for necessary utility services on the demised premises shall be made in the name of Lessee only, and Lessee shall be solely liable for utility charges as they become due, including those for sewer, water, gas, electricity, and telephone services.

8. ENTRY AND INSPECTION. Lessee shall permit Lessor or Lessor's agents to enter upon the premises at reasonable times and upon reasonable notice, for the purpose of inspecting the same, and will permit Lessor at any time within sixty (60) days prior to the expiration of this lease, to place upon the premises any usual "To Let" or "For Lease" signs, and permit persons desiring to lease the same to inspect the premises thereafter.

9. POSSESSION. If Lessor is unable to deliver possession of the premises at the commencement hereof, Lessor shall not be liable for any damage caused thereby, nor shall this lease be void or voidable, but Lessee shall not be liable for any rent until possession is delivered. Lessee may terminate this lease if possession is not delivered within _____ days of the commencement of the term hereof.

10. INDEMNIFICATION OF LESSOR. Lessor shall not be liable for any damage or injury to Lessee, or any other person, or to any property, occurring on the demised premises or any part thereof, and Lessee agrees to hold Lessor harmless from any claim for damages, no matter how caused.

11. DESTRUCTION OF PREMISES. In the event of a partial destruction of the premises during the term hereof, from any cause, Lessor shall forthwith repair the same, provided that such repairs can be made within sixty (60) days under existing governmental laws and regulations, but such partial destruction shall not terminate this lease, except that Lessee shall be entitled to a proportionate reduction of rent while such repairs are being made, based upon the extent to which the making of such repairs shall interfere with the business of Lessee on the premises. If such repairs cannot be made within said sixty (60) days, Lessor, at his option, may make the same within a reasonable time, this lease continuing in effect with the rent proportionately abated as aforesaid, and in the event that Lessor shall not elect to make such repairs which cannot be made within sixty (60) days, this lease may be terminated at the option of either party. In the event that the building in which the demised premises may be situated is destroyed to an extent of not less than one-third of the replacement costs thereof, Lessor may elect to terminate this lease whether the demised premises be injured or not. A total destruction of the building in which the premises may be situated shall terminate this lease.

12. LESSOR'S REMEDIES ON DEFAULT. If Lessee defaults in the payment of rent, or any additional rent, or defaults in the performance of any of the other covenants or conditions hereof, Lessor may give Lessee notice of such default, and if Lessee does not cure any such default within _____ days after the giving of such notice (or if such other default is of such nature that it cannot

be completely cured within such period, if Lessee does not commence such curing within such days and thereafter proceed with reasonable diligence and in good faith to cure such default), then Lessor may terminate this lease on not less than   days' notice to Lessee. On the date specified in such notice the term of this lease shall terminate, and Lessee shall then quit and surrender the premises to Lessor, but Lessee shall remain liable as hereinafter provided. If this lease shall have been so terminated by Lessor, Lessor may at any time thereafter resume possession of the premises by any lawful means and remove Lessee or other occupants and their effects. No failure to enforce any term shall be deemed a waiver.

13.   SECURITY DEPOSIT. Lessee shall deposit with Lessor on the signing of this lease the sum of
Dollars ($) as security deposit for the performance of Lessee's obligations under this lease, including without limitation the surrender of possession of the premises to Lessor as herein provided. If Lessor applies any part of the deposit to cure any default of Lessee, Lessee shall on demand deposit with Lessor the amount so applied so that Lessor shall have the full deposit on hand at all times during the term of this lease.

14.   TAX INCREASE. In the event there is any increase during any year of the term of this lease in the City, County or Provincial real estate taxes over and above the amount of such taxes assessed for the tax year during which the term of this lease commences, whether because of increased rate or valuation, Lessee shall pay to Lessor upon presentation of paid tax bills an amount equal to   % of the increase in taxes upon the land and building in which the leased premises are situated. In the event that such taxes are assessed for a tax year extending beyond the term of the lease, the obligation of Lessee shall be proportionate to the portion of the lease term included in such year.

15.   COMMON AREA EXPENSES. In the event the demised premises are situated in a shopping center or in a commercial building in which there are common areas, Lessee agrees to pay his pro-rata share of maintenance, taxes, and insurance for the common area.

16.   LAWYER'S FEES. In case suit should be brought for recovery of the premises, or for any sum due hereunder, or because of any act which may arise out of the possession of the premises, by either party, the prevailing party shall be entitled to all costs incurred in connection with such action, including a reasonable lawyer's fee.

17.   WAIVER. No failure of Lessor to enforce any term hereof shall be deemed to be a waiver.

18.   NOTICES. Any notice which either party may give, or is required to give, shall be given by mailing the same, postage prepaid, to Lessee at the premises, or Lessor at the address first written, or at such other places as may be designated by the parties from time to time.

19.   HEIRS, ASSIGNS, SUCCESSORS. This lease is binding upon and inures to the benefit of the heirs, assigns and successors in interest to the parties.

20. OPTION TO RENEW. Provided that Lessee is not in default in the performance of this lease, Lessee shall have the option to renew the lease for an additional term of _____ months commencing at the expiration of the initial lease term. All of the terms and conditions of the lease shall apply during the renewal term except that the monthly rent shall be the sum of $ _____. The option shall be exercised by written notice given to Lessor not less than _____ days prior to the expiration of the initial lease term. If notice is not given in the manner provided herein within the time specified, this option shall expire.

21. SUBORDINATION. This lease is and shall be subordinated to all existing and future liens and encumbrances against the property.

22. ENTIRE AGREEMENT. The foregoing constitutes the entire agreement between the parties and may be modified only in writing signed by both parties. The following Exhibits, if any, have been made a part of this lease before the parties' execution hereof:

Executed under seal on _____.
(date)

Signed, sealed, and)
delivered in the presence)
of)
)

_____   _____ s
Witness for the Landlord   The Landlord

_____   _____ s
Witness for the Tenant   The Tenant

CONFIDENTIALITY AGREEMENT

AGREEMENT and acknowledgement between first party,

(Company) and second party,

(Undersigned).

Whereas, the Company agrees to furnish the Undersigned access to certain confidential information relating to the affairs of the Company solely for purposes of:

Whereas, the Undersigned agrees to review, examine, inspect or obtain such information only for the purposes described above, and to otherwise hold such information confidential and secret pursuant to the terms of this agreement.

BE IT KNOWN, that the Company has or shall furnish to the Undersigned certain confidential information, described on attached list, and may further allow suppliers, customers, employees or representatives of the Company to disclose information to the Undersigned, only upon the following conditions:

1. The Undersigned agrees to hold all confidential or proprietary information or trade secrets ("information") in trust and confidence and agrees that it shall be used only for the contemplated purpose, and shall not be used for any other purpose or disclosed to any third party under any circumstances whatsoever.

2. No copies may be made or retained of any written information supplied.

3. At the conclusion of our discussions, or upon demand by the Company, all information, including written notes, photographs, or memoranda shall be promptly returned to the Company. Undersigned shall retain no copies or written documentation relating thereto.

4. This information shall not be disclosed to any employee, consultant or third party unless said party agrees to execute and be bound by the terms of this agreement, and disclosure by Company is first approved.

5. It is understood that the Undersigned shall have no obligation with respect to any information known by the Undersigned or as may be generally known within the industry prior to date of this agreement, or that shall become common knowledge within the industry thereafter.

6. The Undersigned acknowledges the information disclosed herein is proprietary or trade secrets and, in the event of any breach, the Company shall be entitled to injunctive relief as a cumulative and not necessarily successive or exclusive remedy to a claim for monetary damages.

7. This agreement shall be binding upon and inure to the benefit of the parties, their successors and assigns.

8. This constitutes the entire agreement.

Signed this _____ day of _____, 20___.

Witnessed:

_____   _____
Witness   First Party, for the Company

_____   _____
Witness   Second Party

CONFIRMATION OF VERBAL AGREEMENT

Date:

To:

      This letter is to confirm our agreement, made _____, 20___, to pay your overdue balance of $_____ according to the following terms:

      If this letter does not conform to our agreement, please inform us immediately.

      We understand your financial difficulties and, to accommodate you, will accept payments on these extended terms provided each payment is punctually made when due.

      While this balance remains outstanding we shall ship you C.O.D. and, of course, grant to you all cash discounts on your purchases.

      We are pleased this matter could be resolved on terms satisfactory to us both, and we look forward to your payments and continued patronage.

      Very truly,

_____

CONFIRMATION OF VERBAL ORDER

Date:

To:

Dear   :

    This letter shall confirm your acceptance of our verbal order of   , 20   .

    A copy of our confirmatory purchase order containing the stated terms is enclosed as Purchase Order No.:

    Unless we receive written objection within ten (10) days of your receipt of this order, we shall consider the order confirmed on its terms and shall anticipate delivery of all ordered goods on the date indicated.

    Thank you for your cooperation.

                                            Very truly yours,

                                            _____

CONFLICT OF INTEREST DECLARATION

Employee:

Company:

I acknowledge that I have read the Company policy statement concerning conflicts of interest and I hereby declare that neither I, nor any other business with which I may be associated, nor, to the best of my knowledge, any member of my immediate family, has any conflict between our personal affairs or interests and the proper performance of my responsibilities for the Company that would constitute a violation of that Company policy. Furthermore, I declare that, during my employment, I shall continue to maintain my affairs in accordance with the requirements of said policy.

_____
Employee's Signature

_____
Date

CONSENT FOR DRUG/ALCOHOL SCREEN TESTING

If you are offered and accept employment with _____ (company), in the interest of safety for all concerned, you will be required to take a urine test for drug and/or alcohol use.

I, _____, have been fully informed of the reason for this urine test for drug and/or alcohol (I understand what I am being tested for), the procedure involved, and do hereby freely give my consent. In addition, I understand that the results of this test will be forwarded to my potential employer and become part of my record.

If this test is positive, and for this reason I am not hired, I understand that I will be given the opportunity to explain the results of this test.

I hereby authorize these test results to be released to _____ (company name).

Signature _____   Date _____

Witness _____   Date _____

CONSENT TO ASSIGNMENT

The undersigned, _____, as _____ under a certain contract dated _____, 20___, executed at _____, hereby consents to the assignment of the rights and obligations of _____ as _____ under said contract to _____, Assignee.

Date:

_____
Signature of Assignor

CONSENT TO PARTIAL ASSIGNMENT

The undersigned, _____, hereby consents to the assignment by _____, Assignor, of the sum of _____ Dollars ($_____), which constitutes a portion of the amount due from me to him or her on completion of the performance of his or her obligation under a certain contract for _____, between myself and _____, Assignor, to _____, Assignee.

Date: _____ _____
                                                                                                                Creditor

CONSENT TO RELEASE OF INFORMATION

To:

From: Personnel Office

A request for verification of employment information has been received from:

Please check below those items for which information may be released.

    _____ Salary

    _____ Position

    _____ Department

    _____ Supervisor

    _____ Health records

    _____ Dates of employment

    _____ Part-time/Full-time

    _____ Hours worked

    _____ Whether you work under a maiden name

    _____ Wage attachments

    _____ Reason for separation

    _____ Other:

_____   _____
Employee Signature   Date

    Please return this form to the personnel office as soon as possible. Your consent on this occasion will not constitute a consent to release on future occasions.

CONSIGNMENT AGREEMENT

Agreement made this   day of   , 20   , by and between   (Consignor) and   (Customer).

1. Customer acknowledges receipt of goods as described on annexed schedule. Said goods shall remain property of Consignor until sold. Consignor may from time to time ship additional consigned goods as ordered.

2. The Customer at its own cost and expense agrees to keep and display the goods only in its place of business, and agrees, on demand made before any sale, to return the same in good order and condition. Customer may at its own election return goods to Consignor.

3. The Customer agrees to use its best efforts to sell the goods for the Consignor's account on cash terms, and at such prices as shall from time to time be set by Consignor, and at no lesser price.

4. The Customer agrees, upon sale, to maintain proceeds due Consignor in trust, and separate and apart from its own funds and deliver such proceeds, less commission, to Consignor together with an accounting within   days of said sale.

5. The Customer agrees to accept as full payment a commission equal to   % of the gross sales price (exclusive of any sales tax), which the Customer shall collect and remit.

6. The Customer agrees to permit the Consignor to enter the premises at reasonable times to examine and inspect the goods, and reconcile an accounting of sums due.

7.	Customer acknowledges that title to the goods shall remain with Consignor until goods are sold in the ordinary course of business.

8.	Risk of loss of the goods shall be the responsibility of Customer while said goods are within its possession.

9.	This agreement may be terminated by either party at will. Upon termination all unsold goods shall be returned together with payment of any monies due.

10.	This agreement is not assignable and shall not be modified except by written modification.

11.	This agreement shall be binding upon and inure to the benefit of the parties, their successors, assigns and personal representatives.

_____   _____
Consignor   Customer (Consignee)

CONSULTING SERVICES AGREEMENT

The parties to this agreement are the following:

Consultant:

Client:

The consultant will consult with and advise in the following matters:

FEES & EXPENSES:

The consultant's fee for the above services is $

based upon an estimated duration of   .

A retainer of $ is immediately due and payable. Future payments will be made upon completion of this assignment, or in exchange for the documents provided.

Expenses will be reimbursed upon receipt of the invoice.

Signed this   day of   , 20   .

_____   _____
Consultant   Client

CONTRACT

Agreement made this _____ day of _____, 20___, between _____, hereinafter _____, and _____, hereinafter _____.

The parties to this agreement, in consideration of the mutual covenants and stipulations set out, agree as follows:

SECTION I

INSTRUMENT AS ENTIRE AGREEMENT

This instrument contains the entire agreement between the parties, and no statements, promises, or inducements made by either party or agent of either party that are not contained in this contract shall be valid or binding; this contract may not be enlarged, modified, or altered except in writing signed by both parties and endorsed on this agreement.

SECTION II

EFFECT OF AGREEMENT

This agreement shall inure to the benefit of and be binding on the heirs, executors, assignees, and successors of the respective parties.

IN WITNESS WHEREOF, the parties have executed this agreement on the day and year first above written.

_____ _____
Signature of First Party   Signature of Second Party

_____ _____
Print Name of First Party   Print Name of Second Party

_____ _____
Address of First Party   Address of Second Party

CREDIT INFORMATION REQUEST

Date:

To:

Dear

Thank you for your recent order dated _____ , 20___ .

We shall be pleased to consider you for a line of credit, however, we first require additional information.

Accordingly, would you please provide us with the information checked?

_____ Bank Affiliations

_____ Credit Application (enclosed)

_____ Current Financial Statements

_____ (   ) Trade References and Bank References

_____ Dun and Bradstreet or Other Credit Reporting Rating

_____ Other:

Pending receipt of this information we suggest C.O.D. or advance payment of $_____ on this order to expedite prompt shipment. Upon receipt we shall immediately ship your order.

A self-addressed return envelope is enclosed for your convenience. Of course, all credit information submitted shall be held in strict confidence.

Very truly yours,

_____

CREDIT INTERCHANGE

Date:

To:

Re:

Dear

    This letter is in reply to your request for credit information on the above captioned account. Accordingly, we submit the following information:

1.   We have sold the account since_____

2.   The account's present balance is:

        Under 30 days $_____

        30-60 days $_____

        60-90 days $_____

        Over 90 days $_____

        Total Owed $_____

3.   We currently ship the account on the following credit terms:

4.   Other credit information:

    We are pleased we could be of service to you and trust this information shall be held in strict confidence.

                                              Very truly yours,

                                              _____

DECLARATION OF TRUST

This declaration of trust is made on   , 20   , by   ("Trustee") in favor of   ("Beneficiary").

The Trustee solemnly declares that he or she holds   ("Property") in trust solely for the benefit of said Beneficiary.

The Trustee further promises the Beneficiary:

(a)   not to deal with the Property in any way, except to transfer it to the Beneficiary, without the authorization of the Beneficiary; and,

(b)   to account to the Beneficiary for any money received by the Trustee, other than from Beneficiary, in connection with holding said Property.

Signed in the presence of:

_____   _____
Witness   Trustee

DEFECTIVE GOODS NOTICE

Date:

To:

Dear

    Please be advised we are in receipt of goods shipped to us under your Invoice or Order No. _____, dated _____, 20____.

    Certain goods as listed on the attached sheet are defective or non-conforming to our order for the following reasons:

    Accordingly, we reject said goods and demand credit or adjustment in the amount of $ _____, representing the billed amount for said items. We also intend to re-ship said goods to you at your expense.

    Please confirm the credit and also issue instructions for the return of said goods.

    You are advised by this notice that we reserve such further rights as we may have under applicable law.

    We anticipate your prompt reply.

Very truly yours,

_____

DEMAND FOR CONTRIBUTION

Date:

To:

On _____, 20____, the undersigned made payment in the amount of _____ Dollars ($_____) to _____ for _____.

Said payment is covered by our agreement dated _____, 20____, requiring contribution in the event of _____.

Accordingly, the undersigned makes demand upon you for contribution in the amount of _____ Dollars ($_____).

_____

DEMAND FOR DELIVERY

Date:

To:

Dear

    The undersigned has made full payment to you in the sum of $ for certain goods to be shipped by you pursuant to our accepted order dated   , 20   . We demand delivery of said goods in accordance with our order, since said goods have not been received as per terms of our order.

    Unless said goods are received by us on or before   , 20   , we shall consider you to be in breach of contract and we shall thereupon expect a full refund, reserving such further rights as we have under applicable law, for any other damages sustained.

    We shall appreciate immediate notification of your intentions on this matter.

                              Very truly yours,

_____

DEMAND FOR PAYMENT 1

Date:

To:

Dear

    We have tried several times to resolve the problem of your past due account, but the problem continues. Your account remains seriously overdue in the amount of $.

    This is your final notice. Unless we have your cheque for

Dollars $ within ten (10) days, we shall immediately turn your account over to our lawyers for collection.

    We believe you'll agree that immediate payment is in your own best interest as it will save you added interest and court costs, and help preserve your credit rating.

                                                Very truly yours,

                                               _____

DEMAND FOR PAYMENT 2

Date:

To:

Our numerous attempts to resolve your long overdue account have not been successful.

Your failure to make payment on your account may prompt us to take action to collect the account immediately.

Please promptly contact us with an explanation for nonpayment or a payment plan for your overdue account.

Very truly,

_____

DEMAND FOR PAYMENT 3

Date:

To:

Despite our efforts to resolve your past due account, payment on this account has still not been made.

We are informing you that this is your final notice and last opportunity to remit payment.

Unless we have your cheque for $ within the next ten (10) days, we shall immediately turn your account over for collection.

We trust that you will agree that immediate payment is in your own best interest.

Very truly,

_____

DEMAND FOR PAYMENT 4

Date:

To:

We have turned your account over to our (lawyer)(collection agency) to collect your overdue balance of $.

But there remains one final opportunity to resolve your account while avoiding needless additional costs and embarrassment.

If we receive your cheque for $ within the next five (5) days (or reach an acceptable payment arrangement), then we will stop further collection action.

Very truly,

_____

DEMAND FOR RENT

Date:

To:

      Demand is hereby made that you pay to the undersigned _____ Dollars ($_____), which represents past rent as of _____. This sum shall be paid on or before _____, or the lease agreement between us shall be declared forfeited and I shall begin legal proceedings to recover possession of the demised premises as provided in Section _____ of a certain lease agreement between us dated _____, 20____.

                                                                               _____

DEMAND ON GUARANTOR

Date:

To:

    Please be advised that the undersigned is the holder of your guaranty wherein you have guaranteed to us full payment of all monies due us from   (customer).

    You are hereby advised that said obligation is in default. The present balance due us is $.

    Accordingly, demand is hereby made upon you as a guarantor to fully pay said debt.

    Should payment not be received within seven (7) days, we shall proceed to enforce our rights under your guaranty, and you may incur further costs of collection and lawyers' fees.

Very truly,

_____

DEMAND ON GUARANTOR FOR PAYMENT

Date:

To:

Dear

    The undersigned is the holder of your guaranty dated _____, 20___, wherein you guaranteed the debt owed us by _____.

    Please be advised that said debt is in default. Accordingly, demand is made upon you as a guarantor for full payment on the outstanding debt due us in the amount of $_____.

    In the event payment is not made within _____ ( ) days, we shall proceed to enforce our rights against you under the guaranty. We shall additionally hold you responsible for lawyer's fees, costs of collection and further interest as may accrue.

Very truly yours,

_____
Name

_____
Address

_____

DEMAND PROMISSORY NOTE

$ Date:

      FOR VALUE RECEIVED, the undersigned jointly and severally promise to pay to the order of _____ , the sum of _____ Dollars ($_____), together with interest of _____ % per annum on the unpaid balance. The entire unpaid principal and any accrued interest shall be fully and immediately payable UPON DEMAND of any holder thereof.

      Upon default in making payment within _____ days of demand, and provided this note is turned over for collection, the undersigned agree to pay all reasonable legal fees and costs of collection to the extent permitted by law. This note shall take effect as a sealed instrument and be enforced in accordance with the laws of the payee's province. All parties to this note waive presentment, notice of non-payment, protest and notice of protest, and agree to remain fully bound notwithstanding the release of any party, extension or modification of terms, or discharge of any collateral for this note.

In the presence of:

_____   _____
Witness   Debtor

_____   _____
Witness   Debtor

DEMAND TO ENDORSER FOR PAYMENT

Date:

To:

    Please be advised that the undersigned is the holder of the below described instrument on which you are an endorser.

        Maker:

        Date:

        Face Amount:

    Notice is hereby provided that said instrument has been dishonored and has not been paid, and protest and demand is hereby made upon you to immediately pay the amount due in the amount of $.

    In the event payment is not made within five days, the undersigned shall commence suit on your warranties of endorsement.

    Upon full payment on your endorsement, we shall assign to you all our rights, title and interest as we have to the instrument.

                            Very truly yours,

                            _____

REGISTERED MAIL

DEMAND TO PAY PROMISSORY NOTE

Date:

To:

Dear

    Reference is made to a certain promissory note dated   , 20   in the original principal amount of $ and to which the undersigned is holder.

    You are in default under said note in that the following payment(s) have not been made.

    Payment Date   Amount Due

    Accordingly, demand is hereby made for full payment of the entire balance of $ due under the note. In the event payment is not received within   days, this note shall be forwarded to our lawyers for collection and you shall additionally be liable for all reasonable costs of collection.

                                      Very truly yours,

                                      _____

DIRECT DEPOSIT AUTHORIZATION

Name:_____

I.D.#_____

S.I.#_____

Bank Name & Branch:_____

Account Number:_____

Check appropriate box:

_____ Direct deposit.

The undersigned hereby requests and authorizes the entire amount of my paycheque each pay period to be deposited directly into the bank account named above.

_____ Direct payroll deduction deposit.

The undersigned hereby requests and authorizes the sum of _____ _____ Dollars ($_____) be deducted from my paycheque each pay period and to be deposited directly into the bank account named above.

_____ I would like to cancel my deposit authorization.

The undersigned hereby cancels the authorization for direct deposit or payroll deduction deposit previously submitted.

Employee Signature_____Date_____

Please attach a copy of deposit slip.

DISCIPLINARY NOTICE

Employee: _____ Department: _____

Written Warning (   )   Final Warning (   )

1. Statement of the problem (violation of rules, policies, standards or practices, or unsatisfactory performance):

2. Prior, if any, discussion or warnings on this subject, whether oral or written (list dates):

3. Company policy on this subject:

4. Summary of corrective action to be taken by the company and/or employee:

5. Consequences of failure to improve performance or correct behavior:

6. Employee statement (continue on reverse, if necessary):

_____   _____
Supervisor   Date

_____   _____
Employee   Date

DISHONORED CHEQUE PLACED FOR BANK COLLECTION

Date:
To:

Dear

We hereby enclose and place with you for collection and credit to our account the below described cheque previously returned to us due to insufficient/uncollected funds:

    Maker:

    Date of Cheque:

    Cheque Number:

    Amount:

    Drawee Bank:

Please charge our account your customary service fee for handling this cheque on a collection basis.

We would appreciate notification when the cheque clears, or prompt return of said cheque to us should the cheque remain unpaid beyond the collection period.

Thank you for your cooperation.

                                      Very truly yours,

                                      _____

DISPUTED ACCOUNT SETTLEMENT

Settlement Agreement by and between

of _____ (Creditor) and

of _____ (Debtor).

Whereas, Creditor asserts to hold a certain claim against Debtor in the amount of $ _____ arising from the below described transaction:

And whereas, Debtor disputes said claim, and denies said debt is due.

And whereas, the parties desire to resolve and forever settle and adjust said claim.

Now, therefore, Debtor agrees to pay to Creditor and Creditor agrees to accept from Debtor simultaneous herewith, the sum of $ _____ in full payment, settlement, satisfaction, discharge and release of said claim and in release of any further claims thereto. Creditor acknowledges that there shall be no adverse report filed against Debtor with any credit bureau.

This agreement shall be binding upon and inure to the benefit of the parties, their successors, assigns and personal representatives.

Signed this _____ day of _____, 20____.

Witnesseth:

_____   _____
Witness   Creditor

_____   _____
Witness   Debtor

EMPLOYEE AGREEMENT ON INVENTIONS AND PATENTS

Agreement made between _____, hereinafter referred to as "Company," and _____, hereinafter referred to as "Employee."

In consideration of the employment of Employee by Company, the parties agree as follows:

1. Employee shall or may have possession of or access to facilities, apparatus, equipment, drawings, systems, formulae, reports, manuals, invention records, customer lists, computer programs, or other material embodying trade secrets or confidential technical or business information of Company or its Affiliates. Employee therein agrees not to use any such information or material for himself or others, and not to take any such material or reproductions thereof from Company, at any time during or after employment by Company, except as required in Employee's duties to Company. Employee agrees immediately to return all such material and reproductions thereof in his possession to Company upon request and in any event upon termination of employment.

2. Except with prior written authorization by Company, Employee agrees not to disclose or publish any trade secret or confidential technical or business information or material of Company or its Affiliates or of another party to whom Company owes an obligation of confidence, at any time during or after employment by Company.

3. Employee shall promptly furnish to Company a complete record of any and all inventions, patents and improvements, whether patentable or not, which he, solely or jointly, may conceive, make, or first disclose during the period of his employment by Company.

4. Employee agrees to and does hereby grant and assign to Company or its nominee employee's entire right, title, and interest in and to inventions, patents and improvements that relate in any way to the actual or anticipated business or activities of Company or its Affiliates, or that are anticipated by or result from any task or work for or on behalf of Company together with any and all domestic and foreign patent rights in such inventions and improvements. To aid Company or its nominee in securing full benefit and protection thereof, Employee agrees promptly to do all lawful acts reasonably requested, at any time during and after employment by Company, without additional compensation but at Company's expense.

5. Employee agrees that, in the event employee accepts employment with any firm or engages in any type of activity in employee's own behalf or in behalf of any organization following termination of his employment with Company, employee shall notify Company in writing within thirty days of the name and address of such organization and the nature of such activity.

6. Employee agrees to give Company timely written notice of any prior employment agreements or patent rights that might conflict with the interests of Company or its Affiliates.

7. No waiver by either party of any breach by the other party of any provision of this Agreement shall be deemed or construed to be a waiver of any succeeding breach of such provision or as a waiver of the provision itself.

8. This Agreement shall be binding upon and pass to the benefit of the successors and assigns of Company and, insofar as the same may be applied thereto, the heirs, legal representatives, and assigns of Employee.

9. This Agreement shall supersede the terms of any prior employment agreement or understanding between Employee and Company. This Agreement may be modified or amended only in writing signed by an executive officer of Company and by Employee.

10. Should any portion of this Agreement be held to be invalid, unenforceable or void, such holding shall not have the effect of invalidating the remainder of this Agreement or any other part thereof, the parties hereby agreeing that the portion so held to be invalid, unenforceable, or void shall, if possible, be deemed amended or reduced in scope.

11. This agreement shall be binding upon and inure to the benefit of the parties, their successors, assigns and personal representatives.

_____   _____
Company Name   Employee's Full Name

                                         Employee acknowledges reading,
                                         understanding, and receiving a
                                         signed copy of this Agreement.

By:_____   _____
   Company Officer or Witness   Employee's Full Signature

EMPLOYEE CHECKOUT RECORD

Employee: Department:

Termination Date:

Complete or return each of the below checked items upon termination.

Item	Returned	Item	Completed
❐ ID Badge	_____	❐ Exit Interview	_____
❐ Company Tools	_____	❐ Expense Reports	_____
❐ Desk/File Keys	_____	❐ Terminations Form	_____
❐ Security Statement	_____	❐ Confidentiality Report	_____
❐ Air Travel Cards	_____	Other:	
❐ Credit Cards	_____	❐	_____
❐ Petty Cash Advances	_____	❐	_____
❐ Expense Accounts	_____	❐	_____
❐ Keys to Premises	_____		
❐ Catalog/Sales Items	_____		
❐ Sample Products	_____		
❐ Vehicles	_____		
❐ Company Documents	_____		
❐ Customer Lists	_____		

Other:

❐ _____

❐ _____

_____   _____
Supervisor   Date

EMPLOYEE CONSULTATION

Employee: Department:

Nature of Problem:

Date of Problem:

Warning: First (   )   Second (   )   Third (   )

Suspension: From: To: Return to Work:

Discharge:

Description of Problem:

Disciplinary Action to be Taken:

Employee Statement:

_____   _____
Supervisor   Date

_____   _____
Employee   Date

EMPLOYEE COVENANT: EXPENSE RECOVERY

The undersigned, _____ (Employee), of _____ (Employer), hereby promises the Employer:

To reimburse the Employer all amounts paid by the Employer to the Employee as compensation for or reimbursement of expenses incurred in the course of employment that are disallowed, in whole or in part, as deductible to the Employer for income tax purposes.

Date:

Signed in the presence of:

_____   _____
Witness   Employee

EMPLOYEE EXIT INTERVIEW

Employee: Position:

Department: Supervisor:

Employed From: To:

Reason For Termination:

Employee Returned:

_____ keys	_____ safety equipment	_____ tools
_____ ID card	_____ company documents	_____ uniform
_____ credit card	_____ other company property	_____ company vehicle

Employee was informed about restrictions on:

_____ trade secrets   _____ removing company documents

_____ patents   _____ employment with competitor (if applicable)

_____ other

Employee exit questions/answers:

1. Did management adequately recognize your contributions?

2. Did you feel that you had the support of management?

3. Were you properly trained for your job?

4. Was your work rewarding?

5. Were you fairly treated by the company?

6. Was your salary adequate?

7. How were your working conditions?

8. Were you supervised properly?

9. Did you understand all company policies?

10. Have you seen theft of company property?

11. How can the company improve security?

12. How can the company improve working conditions?

13. What do you feel are the company's strengths?

14. What do you feel are the company's weaknesses?

15. Other employee comments or suggestions:

EMPLOYEE INDEMNITY AGREEMENT

In consideration and as an inducement of _____ (Employee) being employed by _____ (Company) as a _____, and in recognition of the Company's reliance on Employee's skill and experience, Company agrees to fully indemnify and save harmless Employee from any claim by any third party alleging neglect or wrongdoing on Employee's part, or loss or expense as a result of any violation of law that was within the scope of Employee's employment to obey. Exempted from this indemnity agreement shall be such claims against which the Company is adequately insured and/or any liability to which the Company or any other employee shares responsibility.

In the event of any asserted claim against Employee and upon reasonable notice of such claim, then Company shall at its own expense defend, indemnify, save harmless and reimburse the Employee for any loss or liability that may arise from such claim.

This indemnity agreement shall be binding upon and inure to the benefit of the parties, their successors, assigns and personal representatives.

Signed under seal this _____ day of _____, 20 ___.

_____
Company

_____
By

Acknowledged:

_____ _____
Employee   Date

EMPLOYEE INFORMATION UPDATE

To All Employees:

Please print all information.

Name:

Street Address:

City:

Province:

Postal Code:

Telephone Number:

Social Insurance Number:

Marital Status:

Name of Spouse:

Number of Dependents:

Emergency Contact:

Emergency Telephone Number:

EMPLOYEE NON-COMPETE AGREEMENT

For good consideration and as an inducement for _____ (Company) to employ _____ (Employee), the undersigned Employee hereby agrees not to directly or indirectly compete with the business of the Company and its successors and assigns during the period of employment and for a period of _____ years following termination of employment and notwithstanding the cause or reason for termination.

The term "not compete" as used herein shall mean that the Employee shall not own, manage, operate, consult to or be employed in a business substantially similar to or competitive with the present business of the Company or such other business activity in which the Company may substantially engage during the term of employment.

The Employee acknowledges that the Company shall or may in reliance of this agreement provide Employee access to trade secrets, customers and other confidential data and that the provisions of this agreement are reasonably necessary to protect the Company and its good will. Employee agrees to retain said information as confidential and not to use said information on his or her own behalf or disclose same to any third party.

This agreement shall be binding upon and inure to the benefit of the parties, their successors, assigns and personal representatives.

Signed this _____ day of _____, 20___.

_____
Company

_____
Employee

EMPLOYEE NON-DISCLOSURE AGREEMENT

FOR GOOD CONSIDERATION, and in consideration of being employed by _____ (Company), the undersigned employee hereby agrees and acknowledges:

1. That during the course of my employment there may be disclosed to me certain trade secrets of the Company, said trade secrets consisting but not necessarily limited to:

    a) Technical information: Methods, processes, formulae, compositions, systems, techniques, inventions, machines, computer programs and research projects.

    b) Business information: Customer lists, pricing data, sources of supply, financial data and marketing, production, or merchandising systems or plans.

2. I agree that I shall not, during, or at any time after the termination of my employment with the Company, use for myself or others, or disclose or divulge to others including future employers, any trade secrets, confidential information, or any other proprietary data of the Company in violation of this agreement.

3. That upon the termination of my employment from the Company:

    a) I shall return to the Company all documents and property of the Company, including but not necessarily limited to: drawings, blueprints, reports, manuals, correspondence, customer lists, computer programs, and all other materials and all copies thereof relating in any way to the Company's business, or in any way obtained by me during the course of employ. I further agree that I shall not retain any copies, notes or abstracts of the foregoing.

    b) The Company may notify any future or prospective employer or third party of the existence of this agreement, and shall be entitled to full injunctive relief for any breach.

    c) This agreement shall be binding upon me and my personal representatives and successors in interest, and shall inure to the benefit of the Company, its successors and assigns.

Signed this _____ day of _____, 20___.

_____   _____
Company   Employee

EMPLOYEE REFERRAL REQUEST

Date:

To:

We consider our employees to be an excellent source for locating other qualified prospective employees.

Please refer individuals known to you who are qualified for any existing or potential vacancy to the undersigned.

Our "employee through employee" candidate referral program is a valuable tool to bring in quality recruits, and to build goodwill among present employees. In addition, as an incentive, for each referral who is subsequently hired and remains with us for a period of   months, the referring employee will receive $.

Thank you for your efforts.

Sincerely,

_____
Personnel Manager

EMPLOYEE RELEASE

IN GOOD CONSIDERATION of employment, the undersigned

(Employee) hereby forever releases, discharges, acquits and forgives
(Company) from any and all claims, actions, suits, demands, agreements, and each of them, if more than one, liabilities, judgments, and proceedings both at law and in equity arising from the beginning of time to the date of these presents and as more particularly related to or arising from said employment.

This release shall be binding upon and inure to the benefit of the parties, their successors, assigns and personal representatives.

Signed this _____ day of _____, 20____.

_____
Employee

In the presence of:

_____
Witness

EMPLOYEE SALARY RECORD

Employee: _____

Starting Date: _____   Starting Salary: _____

Position	Increase Date	Increase	Type of Increase (merit/promotion/ COL/etc.)
_____	_____	_____	_____
_____	_____	_____	_____
_____	_____	_____	_____
_____	_____	_____	_____
_____	_____	_____	_____
_____	_____	_____	_____
_____	_____	_____	_____
_____	_____	_____	_____
_____	_____	_____	_____
_____	_____	_____	_____
_____	_____	_____	_____
_____	_____	_____	_____
_____	_____	_____	_____
_____	_____	_____	_____
_____	_____	_____	_____
_____	_____	_____	_____
_____	_____	_____	_____
_____	_____	_____	_____
_____	_____	_____	_____

EMPLOYEE WARNING

Date:

To: (Employee)

You are hereby advised that your work performance is unsatisfactory for the following reasons:

We expect immediate correction of the problem otherwise we shall have no alternative but to consider termination of your employment.

If there is any question about this notice, or if we can help you improve your performance or correct the difficulties, then please discuss this matter with your supervisor at the earliest possible opportunity.

_____

EMPLOYEE'S AGREEMENT ON CONFIDENTIAL DATA

I, the undersigned, _____, acknowledge that I have received all salary, earnings and other compensation due me during my employment by the Company, which terminated on _____, 20___. I certify that I have not done, or in any way been a party to, or knowingly permitted:

1. Disclosure of any confidential matters or trade secrets of the Company.

2. Retention or copying of any confidential materials or documents issued to or used by me or others during my employment.

I acknowledge that I have again been carefully and fully advised by the Company of my continuing obligations to preserve as confidential, and not to reveal to anyone or use, for myself or anyone else, any trade secrets or confidential matters learned by me during, or by reason of, my employment by the Company, and I reaffirm such obligations. I agree that the Company may inform my new employer, in writing, of my said obligations, provided only that I receive a copy of such letter or other related communication.

_____   _____
Employee   Date

EMPLOYMENT AGREEMENT

Employment Agreement, between _____ (the "Company") and _____ (the "Employee").

1. FOR GOOD CONSIDERATION, the Company employs the Employee on the following terms and conditions.

2. TERM OF EMPLOYMENT. Subject to the provisions for termination set forth below this agreement will begin on _____ , 20___ , unless sooner terminated.

3. SALARY. The Company shall pay Employee a salary of $ _____ per year, for the services of the Employee, payable at regular payroll periods.

4. DUTIES AND POSITION. The Company hires the Employee in the capacity of _____ . The Employee's duties may be reasonably modified at the Company's discretion from time to time.

5. EMPLOYEE TO DEVOTE FULL TIME TO COMPANY. The Employee will devote full time, attention, and energies to the business of the Company, and, during this employment, will not engage in any other business activity, regardless of whether such activity is pursued for profit, gain, or other pecuniary advantage. Employee is not prohibited from making personal investments in any other businesses provided those investments do not require active involvement in the operation of said companies.

6. CONFIDENTIALITY OF PROPRIETARY INFORMATION. Employee agrees, during or after the term of this employment, not to reveal confidential information or trade secrets to any person, firm, corporation, or entity. Should Employee reveal or threaten to reveal this information, the Company shall be entitled to an injunction restraining the Employee from disclosing same, or from rendering any services to any entity to whom said information has been or is threatened to be disclosed. The right to secure an injunction is not exclusive, and the Company may pursue any other remedies it has against the Employee for a breach or threatened breach of this condition, including the recovery of damages from the Employee.

7. REIMBURSEMENT OF EXPENSES. The Employee may incur reasonable expenses for furthering the Company's business, including expenses for entertainment, travel, and similar items. The Company shall reimburse Employee for all business expenses after the Employee presents an itemized account of expenditures, pursuant to Company policy.

8. VACATION. The Employee shall be entitled to a yearly vacation of _____ weeks at full pay.

9. DISABILITY. If Employee cannot perform the duties because of illness or incapacity for a period of more than _____ weeks, the compensation otherwise due during said illness or incapacity will be reduced by _____ (___) percent. The Employee's full compensation

will be reinstated upon return to work. However, if the Employee is absent from work for any reason for a continuous period of over   months, the Company may terminate the Employee's employment, and the Company's obligations under this agreement will cease on that date.

10. TERMINATION OF AGREEMENT. Without cause, the Company may terminate this agreement at any time upon   days' written notice to the Employee. If the Company requests, the Employee will continue to perform his/her duties and be paid his/her regular salary up to the date of termination. In addition, the Company will pay the Employee on the date of termination a severance allowance of $ less taxes and Social Insurance required to be withheld. Without cause, the Employee may terminate employment upon   days written notice to the Company. Employee may be required to perform his or her duties and will be paid the regular salary to date of termination but shall not receive a severance allowance. Notwithstanding anything to the contrary contained in this agreement, the Company may terminate the Employee's employment upon   days' notice to the Employee should any of the following events occur:

    a) The sale of substantially all of the Company's assets to a single purchaser or group of associated purchasers; or

    b) The sale, exchange, or other disposition, in one transaction, of the majority of the Company's outstanding corporate shares; or

    c) The Company's decision to terminate its business and liquidate its assets; or

    d) The merger or consolidation of the Company with another company; or

    e) Bankruptcy.

11. DEATH BENEFIT. Should Employee die during the term of employment, the Company shall pay to Employee's estate any compensation due through the end of the month in which death occurred.

12. RESTRICTION ON POST EMPLOYMENT COMPETITION. For a period of   (   ) years after the end of employment, the Employee shall not control, consult to or be employed by any business similar to that conducted by the Company, either by soliciting any of its accounts or by operating within Employer's general trading area.

13. ASSISTANCE IN LITIGATION. Employee shall upon reasonable notice, furnish such information and proper assistance to the Company as it may reasonably require in connection with any litigation in which it is, or may become, a party either during or after employment.

14. EFFECT OF PRIOR AGREEMENTS. This agreement supersedes any prior agreement between the Company or any predecessor of the Company and the Employee, except that this agreement shall not affect or operate to reduce any benefit or compensation inuring to the Employee of a kind elsewhere provided and not expressly provided in this agreement.

15. SETTLEMENT BY ARBITRATION. Any claim or controversy that arises out of or relates to this agreement, or the breach of it, shall be settled by arbitration. Judgment upon the award rendered may be entered in any court with jurisdiction.

16. LIMITED EFFECT OF WAIVER BY COMPANY. Should Company waive breach of any provision of this agreement by the Employee, that waiver will not operate or be construed as a waiver of further breach by the Employee.

17. SEVERABILITY. If, for any reason, any provision of this agreement is held invalid, all other provisions of this agreement shall remain in effect. If this agreement is held invalid or cannot be enforced, then to the full extent permitted by law any prior agreement between the Company (or any predecessor thereof) and the Employee shall be deemed reinstated as if this agreement had not been executed.

18. ASSUMPTION OF AGREEMENT by Company's Successors and Assignees. The Company's rights and obligations under this agreement will inure to the benefit and be binding upon the Company's successors and assignees.

19. ORAL MODIFICATIONS NOT BINDING. This instrument is the entire agreement of the Company and the Employee. Oral changes shall have no effect. It may be altered only by a written agreement signed by the party against whom enforcement of any waiver, change, modification, extension, or discharge is sought.

Signed this _____ day of _____, 20___.

_____   _____
Witness   Company Representative

_____   _____
Witness   Employee

EMPLOYMENT APPLICATION
(please print)

Full Name: _____

Address: _____

City: _____ Province: _____ Postal: _____

Phone: _____ Social Insurance No: _____

Position Applied For: _____

Are you a citizen of Canada?   ❏ Yes   ❏ No

Are you legally entitled to work? _____

Do you voluntarily identify yourself as a veteran for reporting purposes? ❏ Yes ❏ No

EDUCATION
(name and location of school)

High School: _____

_____

Did you graduate? _____ Degree: _____

Bus./Trade: _____

_____

Did you graduate? _____ Degree: _____

Col./Univ.: _____

Did you graduate? _____ Degree: _____

Grad./Prof.: _____

Did you graduate? _____ Degree: _____

PREVIOUS EMPLOYMENT
(begin with most recent position)

Most Recent

Firm: _____ Address: _____

Supervisor: _____ Nature of Business: _____

Dates of Employment: _____ Position(s) Held: _____

Ending Salary: _____ Reason for Leaving: _____

Previous Employer

Firm: _____ Address: _____

Supervisor: _____ Nature of Business: _____

Dates of Employment: _____ Position(s) Held: _____

Ending Salary: _____ Reason for Leaving: _____

Previous Employer

Firm: _____ Address: _____

Supervisor: _____ Nature of Business: _____

Dates of employment: _____ Position(s) Held: _____

Ending Salary: _____ Reason for Leaving: _____

REFERENCES

Please furnish the names and addresses of two people to whom you are not related and by whom you have not been employed.

Name: _____

Address: _____

Name: _____

Address: _____

Who referred you to us? (person or agency): _____

_____

Summarize your special skills or qualifications:

_____

_____

_____

    I certify that my answers are true and complete to the best of my knowledge.

    I authorize you to make such investigations and inquiries of my personal, employment, educational, financial, or medical history and other related matters as may be necessary for an employment decision. I hereby release employers, schools, or persons from all liability in responding to inquiries in connection with my application.

    In the event I am employed, I understand that false or misleading information given in my application or interview(s) may result in discharge.

Signature of Applicant: _____ Date: _____

For Department Use Only

Action: _____

_____

_____

EMPLOYMENT APPLICATION DISCLAIMER AND ACKNOWLEDGEMENT

I certify that the information contained in this application is correct to the best of my knowledge. I understand that to falsify information is grounds for refusing to hire me, or for discharge should I be hired.

I authorize any person, organization or company listed on this application to furnish you any and all information concerning my previous employment, education and qualifications for employment. I also authorize you to request and receive such information.

In consideration for my employment, I agree to abide by the rules and regulations of the company, which rules may be changed, withdrawn, added or interpreted at any time, at the company's sole option and without prior notice to me.

I also acknowledge that my employment may be terminated, or any offer, or acceptance of employment withdrawn, at any time, with or without cause, and with or without prior notice at the option of the company or myself.

Signature: _____   Date: _____

EMPLOYMENT CHANGES

Employee: _____ Employment Date: _____

Department: _____ Supervisor: _____

Effective Date: _____ Date Submitted: _____

1. Pay Rate Change:

    From: _____ to _____

2. Position Title Change:

    From: _____ to _____

3. Position Classification Change:

    From: _____ to _____

4. Shift Change:

    From: _____ to _____

5. Full-Time/Part-Time Change:

    From: _____ to _____

6. Temporary/Permanent Change:

    From: _____ to _____

7. Other: (Describe)

    _____

    _____

_____   _____
Submitted By   Date

_____   _____
Approved By   Date

EXCEPTIONS TO PURCHASE ORDER

Date:

To:

Dear   :

We are in receipt of your Purchase Order No.   dated   , 20   .

We confirm acceptance of said order subject only to the following exceptions:

On exceptions noted, we shall assume you agree to same unless objection is received within ten (10) days of your receipt of this notice. We shall promptly ship such goods as are not subject to exception.

Thank you for your business, and we trust you understand the reasons for the exceptions.

Very truly yours,

_____

EXCLUSIVE RIGHT TO SELL

For and in consideration of your services to be rendered in listing for sale and in undertaking to sell or find a purchaser for the property hereinafter described, the parties understand and agree that this is an exclusive listing to sell the real estate located at:

,

together with the following improvements and fixtures:

The minimum selling price of the property shall be
Dollars ($), to be payable on the following terms:

You are authorized to accept and hold a deposit in the amount of
Dollars ($) as a deposit and to apply such deposit on the purchase price.

If said property is sold, traded or in any other way disposed of either by us or by anyone else within the time specified in this listing, it is agreed to and understood that you shall receive from the sale or trade of said property as your commission   percent (%) of the purchase price. Should said property be sold or traded within   days after expiration of this listing agreement to a purchaser with whom you have been negotiating for the sale or trade of the property, the said commission shall be due and payable on demand.

We agree to furnish a certificate of title showing a good and merchantable title of record, and further agree to convey by good and sufficient warranty deed or guaranteed title on payment in full.

This listing contract shall continue until midnight of   , 20   .

Date:

_____
Owner

_____
Owner

I accept this listing and agree to act promptly and diligently to procure a buyer for said property.

Date:

_____

EXERCISE OF OPTION

Date:

To:

You are hereby notified that the undersigned has elected to and does hereby exercise and accept the option dated _____, 20___, executed by you as seller to the undersigned as purchaser, and agrees to all terms, conditions, and provisions of the option.

_____
Signature of Purchaser

_____
Name of Purchaser

_____
Address of Purchaser

_____

EXTENDED TERM RESCINDED AND DEMAND FOR PAYMENT

Date:

To:

    A payment agreement made _____, 20___, gave you extended terms over ( ) months, provided each payment was punctually made when due.

    You have defaulted on these agreed terms, and are now in arrears $_____, representing (_____) installments. Therefore, we now rescind your rights to extended payments, and demand the entire balance of $_____.

    Please pay the said balance within seven (7) days, otherwise, we shall turn this matter over for collection. This may result in additional costs to you.

    We regret this action is necessary, but expect that you will respond accordingly to settle your account.

    Very truly,

_____

EXTENSION OF AGREEMENT

Extension of Agreement made by and between _____ (First Party), and _____ (Second Party), said agreement being dated _____, 20____ (Agreement).

Whereas said Agreement expires on _____, 20____, and the parties desire to extend and continue said agreement, it is provided that said Agreement shall be extended for an additional term commencing upon the expiration of the original term with the new term expiring on _____, 20____.

This extension shall be on the same terms and conditions as contained in the original agreement and as if set forth and incorporated herein excepting only for the following modification to the original agreement:

This extension of Agreement shall be binding upon and inure to the benefit of the parties, their successors and assigns.

Signed this _____ day of _____, 20____.

In the presence of:

_____   _____
Witness   First Party

_____   _____
Witness   Second Party

EXTENSION OF DEBT PAYMENT AGREEMENT

FOR VALUE RECEIVED, the undersigned 	(Creditor) and 	(Debtor) hereby agree that:

1.	The Debtor presently owes the Creditor the sum of $	, said sum being presently due and payable, but the Debtor is unable to fully pay same at present.

2.	In further consideration of the Creditor's forbearance, the Debtor agrees to pay said debt on extended terms in the following manner:

3.	In the event the Debtor fails to make any payments punctually on the agreed extended terms, the Creditor shall have full rights to proceed for the collection of the entire balance then remaining.

4.	In the event of default in payment the Debtor agrees to pay all reasonable lawyer's fees and costs of collection.

5.	This agreement shall be binding upon and inure to the benefit of the parties, their successors, assigns and personal representatives.

Signed this 	 day of 	, 20 	.

_____
Creditor

_____
Debtor

EXTENSION OF LEASE

Extension of Lease Agreement made by and between _____ (Landlord), and _____ (Tenant) relative to a certain lease agreement for premises known as _____, and dated _____, 20____ . (Lease)

For good consideration, Landlord and Tenant each agree to extend the term of said Lease for a period of _____ years commencing on _____, 20____, and terminating on _____, 20____, with no further right of renewal or extension beyond said termination date.

During the extended term, Tenant shall pay Lessor rent of $_____ per annum, payable _____ ($_____) per month in advance.

Other terms are as follows:

It is further provided, however, that all other terms of the Lease shall continue during this extended term as if set forth herein.

This agreement shall be binding upon and shall inure to the benefit of the parties, their successors, assigns and personal representatives.

Signed this _____ day of _____, 20____ .

Witnessed:

_____   _____
Witness   Landlord

_____   _____
Witness   Tenant

FINAL NOTICE BEFORE LEGAL ACTION

Date:

To:

Dear

    We have repeatedly advised you of your long overdue balance in the amount of $.

    Since you have not made payment, we have turned your account over to our lawyers and instructed them to commence suit without further delay.

    There is still time, however, to avoid suit if you contact us within the next five (5) days.

    This will be your final opportunity to resolve matters without the expense of court proceedings.

                                                   Very truly yours,

                                                   _____

FINAL WARNING BEFORE DISMISSAL

Date:

To:

Dear

You have been previously warned of certain problems in your performance as our employee. These problems include:

There has not been a satisfactory improvement in your performance since your last warning. Accordingly, any continued violations of company policy or failure to perform according to the standards of our company shall result in immediate termination of your employment without further warning.

Please contact the undersigned or your supervisor if you have any questions.

Very truly yours,

_____

FIRST WARNING NOTICE

Employee: _____ Employee No.: _____

Shift: _____ Date of warning: _____

Date of violation: _____ Time of violation: _____

Violation

____ Intoxication or drugs   ____ Substandard work   ____ Disobedience

____ Clocking out ahead of time   ____ Wrongful conduct   ____ Tardiness

____ Clocking out wrong time card   ____ Carelessness   ____ Absenteeism

____ Other: _____

Action Taken: _____

_____

_____

Additional Remarks: _____

_____

_____

Employee Comments: _____

_____

_____

This is your first warning of a company rules violation or unsatisfactory performance. Future violations may lead to immediate dismissal without further notice.

_____
Employee

_____
Supervisor

_____
Personnel Manager

FUNERAL LEAVE REQUEST

Employee: _____ Date: _____

Department: _____

Dates of missed work days: _____ Hourly Rate: _____

Name of Deceased: _____ Funeral Date: _____

Residence (city/town): _____ Province: _____

Burial Place: _____

Relationship to employee: (be specific) _____

_____

_____

Comments: _____

_____

_____

                                                                               _____

                                                                                       Employee

Approved

_____

Supervisor

GENERAL AGREEMENT

THIS AGREEMENT, made this   day of   , 20   , by and between   (First Party) and   (Second Party).

WITNESSETH: That in consideration of the mutual covenants and agreements to be kept and performed on the part of said parties hereto, respectively as herein stated, the said party of the first part does hereby covenant and agree that it shall:

I.

II.   And said party of the second part covenants and agrees that it shall:

III. Other terms to be observed by and between the parties:

This agreement shall be binding upon the parties, their successors, assigns and personal representatives. Time is of the essence on all undertakings. This agreement shall be enforced under the laws of the Province of   . This is the entire agreement.

Signed the day and year first above written.

Signed in the presence of:

_____   _____
Witness   First Party

_____   _____
Witness   Second Party

GENERAL ASSIGNMENT

BE IT KNOWN, for value received, the undersigned   of   hereby unconditionally and irrevocably assigns and transfers unto   of   all right, title and interest in and to the following:

The undersigned fully warrants that it has full rights and authority to enter into this assignment and that the rights and benefits assigned hereunder are free and clear of any lien, encumbrance, adverse claim or interest by any third party.

This assignment shall be binding upon and inure to the benefit of the parties, and their successors and assigns.

Signed this   day of   , 20   .

_____   _____
Witness   Assignor

_____   _____
Witness   Assignee

GENERAL NONDISCLOSURE AGREEMENT

To induce _____ (Client) to retain _____ (Promisor) as an outside consultant and to furnish Promisor with certain information that is proprietary and confidential, Promisor hereby warrants, represents, covenants, and agrees as follows:

1. ENGAGEMENT. Promisor, in the course of engagement by Client, may or will have access to or learn certain information belonging to Client that is proprietary and confidential (Confidential Information).

2. DEFINITION OF CONFIDENTIAL INFORMATION. Confidential Information as used throughout this Agreement means any secret or proprietary information relating directly to Client's business and that of Client's affiliated companies and subsidiaries, including, but not limited to, products, customer lists, pricing policies, employment records and policies, operational methods, marketing plans and strategies, product development techniques or plans, business acquisition plans, new personnel acquisition plans, methods of manufacture, technical processes, designs and design projects, inventions and research programs, trade "know-how," trade secrets, specific software, algorithms, computer processing systems, object and source codes, user manuals, systems documentation, and other business affairs of Client and its affiliated companies and subsidiaries.

3. NONDISCLOSURE. Promisor agrees to keep strictly confidential all Confidential Information and will not, without Client's express written authorization signed by one of Client's authorized officers, use, sell, market, or disclose any Confidential Information to any third person, firm, corporation, or association for any purpose. Promisor further agrees not to make any copies of the Confidential Information except upon Client's written authorization, signed by one of Client's authorized officers, and will not remove any copy or sample of Confidential Information from the premises of Client without such authorization.

4. RETURN OF MATERIAL. Upon receipt of a written request from Client, Promisor will return to Client all copies or samples of Confidential Information that, at the time of the receipt of the notice, are in Promisor's possession.

5. OBLIGATIONS CONTINUE PAST TERM. The obligations imposed on Promisor shall continue with respect to each unit of the Confidential Information following the termination of the business relationship between Promisor and Client, and such obligations shall not terminate until such unit shall cease to be secret and confidential and shall be in the public domain, unless such event shall have occurred as a result of wrongful conduct by Promisor or Promisor's agents, servants, officers, or employees or a breach of the covenants set forth in this Agreement.

6. EQUITABLE RELIEF. Promisor acknowledges and agrees that a breach of the provisions of Paragraph 3 or 4 of this Agreement would cause Client to suffer irreparable damage that could not be adequately remedied by an action at law. Accordingly, Promisor agrees that Client shall have the right to seek specific performance of the provisions of Paragraph 3 to enjoin a breach or attempted breach of the provision thereof, such right being in addition to all other rights and remedies that are available to Client at law, in equity, or otherwise.

7. INVALIDITY. If any provision of this Agreement or its application is held to be invalid, illegal, or unenforceable in any respect, the validity, legality, or enforceability of any of the other provisions and applications therein shall not in any way be affected or impaired.

IN WITNESS WHEREOF, this Agreement has been signed on the _____ day of _____, 20___.

_____ _____
Witness   Promisor

GENERAL SUBORDINATION

     FOR VALUE RECEIVED, the undersigned hereby agrees to subordinate its claims for debts now or hereinafter due the undersigned from _____ (Debtor) , to any and all debts that may now or hereinafter be due

_____ (Creditor), from said Debtor.

     This subordination shall be unlimited as to amount or duration and shall include subordination of all secured obligations together with unsecured obligations.

     This subordination agreement shall be binding upon and inure to the benefit of the parties, their successors, assigns and personal representatives.

     Signed this _____ day of _____, 20___.

_____

Assented to:

_____
Debtor

GRANT OF RIGHT TO USE NAME

In consideration of _____ Dollars ($_____), payable in the following manner:

The undersigned, _____, hereby grants to _____, as grantee, the sole right to use the name:
for a term of _____ year(s), commencing on _____, 20___,
for the purpose of _____.

The undersigned hereby warrants and guarantees that he or she has not and will not during said period of this grant give permission or license to use such name for any business purpose to any other person or entity and that the undersigned will execute all documents and do all things reasonably requested by grantee to give full effect to this agreement.

Dated: _____

_____
Grantor

_____
Grantee

GRIEVANCE FORM

Employee: _____ Date: _____

Department: _____

State your grievance in detail, including the date of aggrieved act(s):

Identify other employees with personal knowledge or observance of your grievance:

State briefly your efforts to resolve this grievance:

Describe the remedy or solution you seek:

_____   _____
Employee   Date

Grievance Team Personnel - Informal Review   Date Received: _____

Actions Taken: _____

_____

Disposition: _____

Employee Grievance Accepted: _____ Employee Appealed: _____

Assigned Team Member: _____

Date Communicated: _____

Grievance Team - Formal Review   Date Received: _____

Actions Taken: _____

_____

Disposition: _____

Employee Grievance Accepted: _____ Employee Appealed: _____

Grievance Review Team: _____

Date Communicated: _____

Grievance Team and Management - Formal Review   Date Received: _____

Actions Taken: _____

_____

Disposition: _____

Employee Grievance Accepted: _____ Employee Appealed: _____

Grievance Review Team: _____

Date Communicated: _____

GUARANTY

FOR GOOD CONSIDERATION, and as an inducement for _____ (Creditor), from time to time extend credit to _____ (Customer), it is hereby agreed that the undersigned does hereby guaranty to Creditor the prompt, punctual and full payment of all monies now or hereinafter due Creditor from Customer.

Until termination, this guaranty is unlimited as to amount or duration and shall remain in full force and effect notwithstanding any extension, compromise, adjustment, forbearance, waiver, release or discharge of any party, obligor, or guarantor, or release in whole or in part of any security granted for said indebtedness or compromise or adjustment thereto, and the undersigned waives all notices thereto.

The obligations of the undersigned shall at the election of Creditor be primary and not necessarily secondary, and Creditor shall not be required to exhaust its remedies as against Customer prior to enforcing its rights under this guaranty against the undersigned.

The guaranty hereunder shall be unconditional and absolute and the undersigned waive all rights of subrogation and set-off until all sums due under this guaranty are fully paid. The undersigned further waives all suretyship defenses or defenses in the nature thereof, generally.

In the event payments due under this guaranty are not punctually paid upon demand, then the undersigned shall pay all reasonable costs and lawyer's fees necessary for collection and enforcement of this guaranty.

If there are two or more guarantors to this guaranty, the obligations shall be joint and several and binding upon and inure to the benefit of the parties, their successors, assigns and personal representatives.

This guaranty may be terminated by any guarantor upon fifteen (15) days written notice of termination, posted by Registered Mail to the Creditor. Such termination shall extend only to credit extended beyond said fifteen (15) day period and not to prior extended credit, or goods in transit received by Customer beyond said date, or for special orders placed prior to said date notwithstanding date of delivery. Termination of this guaranty by any guarantor shall not impair the continuing guaranty of any remaining guarantors of said termination.

Each of the undersigned warrants and represents it has full authority to enter into this guaranty.

This guaranty shall be binding upon and inure to the benefit of the parties, their successors, assigns and personal representatives.

This guaranty shall be construed and enforced under the laws of the Province of   .

Signed this   day of   , 20   .

In the presence of:

_____   _____
Witness   Guarantor

_____   _____
Witness   Guarantor

GUARANTY OF RENTS

FOR GOOD CONSIDERATION and as an inducement for
of   (Landlord) to enter into a lease or tenancy
agreement with   of
(Tenant) for premises at

                                                                                                                                    .

BE IT KNOWN, that the Undersigned do hereby jointly and severally guaranty to the Landlord and his successors and assigns the prompt, punctual and full payment of all rents and other charges that may become due and owing from Tenant to Landlord under said lease or tenancy agreement or any renewal or extension thereof. This guaranty shall also extend or apply to any damages incurred by Landlord for any breach of lease in addition to the failure to pay rents or other charges due under the lease.

Signed this   day of   , 20   .

Witnessed:

_____   _____
Witness   Guarantor

_____   _____
Witness   Guarantor

HELP WANTED ADVERTISING LISTING

Position: _____ Req. #: _____

Department/Division: _____ _____

Charge to Department: _____ _____

Person Requesting Ad: _____ Phone Ext.: _____

Newspaper: _____ _____

Run Ad: _____ (days) _____
         (dates)

Under Classified Heading: _____ _____

Please insert the following ad:

For Department Use Only

Ad Placed: _____ (date) _____ (newspaper)

Cost: $ _____

Ad To Run: _____ (days) _____ (dates)

Re-Run Ordered: _____ (date) _____ (newspaper)

Re-Run Cost: $ _____

Responses:

_____ _____

_____ _____

_____ _____

_____ _____

_____ _____

\

ILLNESS REPORT

Employee: _____ Date: _____

Age: _____ Sex: _____

Department: _____ Supervisor: _____

Is illness related to employment? Yes ( ) No ( )

Date of diagnosis: _____

Describe illness:

_____

_____

_____

If employee left work, time of leaving: _____

If employee returned to work, time of return: _____

Name and address of physician: _____

_____

If hospitalized, name and address of hospital: _____

_____

Comments: _____

_____

_____

_____

_____

_____

_____   _____
Supervisor   Date

INCIDENT REPORT

Employee: _____ Date: _____

Department: _____ Supervisor: _____

Date of incident: _____

Describe incident: _____

_____

_____

_____

Action taken: _____

_____

_____

_____

Witnesses:

Name	Address
_____	_____
_____	_____
_____	_____
_____	_____

Reported to:

Person	Date
_____	_____
_____	_____
_____	_____

Use reverse side for additional remarks.

INDEMNITY AGREEMENT

FOR VALUE RECEIVED, the undersigned jointly and severally agree to indemnify and save harmless _____ (Indemnified) and their successors and assigns, from any claim, action, liability, loss, damage or suit, arising from the following:

In the event of any asserted claim, the Indemnified shall provide the undersigned reasonably timely written notice of same, and thereafter the undersigned shall at its own expense defend, protect and save harmless Indemnified against said claim or any loss or liability thereunder.

In the further event the undersigned shall fail to so defend and/or indemnify and save harmless, then in such instance the Indemnified shall have full rights to defend, pay or settle said claim on their own behalf without notice to undersigned and with full rights to recourse against the undersigned for all fees, costs, expenses and payments made or agreed to be paid to discharge said claim.

Upon default, the undersigned further agree to pay all reasonable lawyer's fees necessary to enforce this agreement.

This agreement shall be unlimited as to amount or duration.

This agreement shall be binding upon and inure to the benefit of the parties, their successors, assigns and personal representatives.

Signed this _____ day of _____, 20___.

Witnessed:

_____   _____
Witness   First Party

INDEPENDENT CONTRACTOR AGREEMENT

Agreement is made this   day of   , 20   .

The following outlines our agreement:

You have been retained by   , as an independent contractor for the project of:

You will be responsible for successfully completing said project according to specifications.

The project is to be completed by   .

The cost to complete will not exceed $.

You will invoice us for your services rendered at the end of each month.

We will not deduct or withhold any taxes or other deductions. As an independent contractor, you will not be entitled to any fringe benefits, such as unemployment insurance, pension plans, or other such benefits that would be offered to regular employees.

During this project you may be in contact with or directly working with proprietary information which is important to our company and its competitive position. All information must be treated with strict confidence and may not be used at any time or in any manner in work you may do with others in our industry.

Agreed:

Independent Contractor_____ Date_____

Company Representative_____ Date_____

INFORMATION REQUEST ON DISPUTED CHARGES

Date:

To:

Dear

Please be advised that we have received your statement of charges, and we dispute certain charges on our account for the following reasons:

We do want to promptly reconcile our account, so we may pay and resolve this matter; however, we find we need the below checked information or documents:

_____	Copies of charges noted on reverse side
_____	Copies of purchase orders
_____	Debit memoranda outstanding
_____	List of goods claimed as shipped
_____	Other: _____

Thank you for your immediate attention. Upon receipt of the requested information we shall give your statement our prompt consideration.

Very truly yours,

_____

INJURY REPORT

Name:_____ Social Insurance No.: _____

Address: _____

_____ Phone:_____

Age: _____ Sex: _____

Is injury related to employment?   Yes (   ) No (   )

Describe:_____

Date of injury: _____ Time of injury: _____

Date of initial diagnosis: _____

Describe the injury in detail and indicate the part of the body affected:

_____

Did employee return to work? Yes (   ) No (   ) If no, indicate last day worked:

_____

Name and address of physician: _____

_____

If hospitalized, name and address of hospital:_____

_____

Names of witnesses:_____

_____

Comments: _____

_____

_____

_____   _____
Employee   Date

_____   _____
Supervisor or first aid person   Date

INSURANCE CLAIM NOTICE

Date:

To:

Dear   :

You are hereby notified that we have incurred a loss covered by insurance you underwrite. The claim information is as follows:

1. Type of Loss or Claim:

2. Date and Time Incurred:

3. Location:

4. Estimated Loss or Casualty:

Please forward a claim form or have an adjuster call me at the below telephone number.

Very truly yours,

_____   _____
Policy Number   Name

                                     _____
                                     Address

                                     _____

_____   _____
Telephone No. (Work)   Telephone No. (Home)

INVITATION TO QUOTE PRICE OF GOODS

Date:

To:

Please quote your ordinary unit price for supplying the following goods together with your discount for volume purchases:

Please also indicate:

(a) whether your quotes are inclusive or exclusive of sales taxes; if not otherwise stated, we will assume your quotes are inclusive of sales taxes;

(b) delivery time from receipt of our purchase order to receipt of your shipment;

(c) if delivery costs are not included in your quote, please state this clearly, otherwise we will assume they are included; if delivery is included, please state the price of goods if we pick up;

(d) your terms of payment.

All price quotations must be firm and state when they expire.

Very truly yours,

_____

LANDLORD'S AND TENANT'S MUTUAL RELEASE

BE IT KNOWN, that _____ of _____ (Landlord) hereby acknowledges that _____ of _____ (Tenant) duly delivered up possession of the premises known as

and Tenant has fully paid all rents due and performed all obligations under said tenancy.

And Tenant acknowledges surrender of said premises as of this date and acknowledges return of any security deposit due from Landlord.

Now, therefore, Landlord and Tenant release and discharge one and the other and their successors and assigns from any and all claims arising under said tenancy.

Signed this _____ day of _____, 20___.

In the presence of:

_____   _____
Witness   Landlord

_____   _____
Witness   Tenant

LANDLORD'S NOTICE TO TERMINATE TENANCY

Date:

To:

    Please be advised that as your landlord you are hereby notified that we intend to terminate your tenancy on the premises you now occupy as our tenant, said premises described as:

    Your tenancy shall be terminated on _____, 20____. We shall require that you deliver to us full possession of the rented premises on said date, free of all your goods and possessions together. We also request all keys to the premises.

    Upon your full compliance, and if applicable, we shall thereupon return any security deposit or escrow we may be holding and that may be due you. Rent for the premises is due and payable through and including the termination date.

    Thank you for your cooperation.

_____
Landlord

_____
Address

_____

REGISTERED MAIL

LANDLORD'S NOTICE TO VACATE

Date:

To:

To the above Tenant and all others now in possession of the below described premises:

You are hereby requested to quit, vacate and deliver possession thereof to the undersigned on or before _____, 20___.

This notice to vacate is due to your following breach of tenancy:

Should you fail, refuse or neglect to pay your rent, cure the breach, or vacate said premises within _____ days from service of this notice, I will take such legal action as the law requires to evict you from the premises. You are to further understand that we shall in all instances hold you responsible for all present and future rents due under your tenancy agreement.

Thank you for your cooperation.

_____

REGISTERED MAIL

LAST WILL AND TESTAMENT OF

This is the Last Will of me, _____,
resident of _____,
_____ (city), _____ (province),
made this ____ day of _____, 2____. I revoke all my prior wills and codicils.

1. I appoint _____,
of _____ (city), _____ (province),
to be my Executor/Executrix and Trustee. If _____ is unwilling or unable to act or to continue to act as my Executor/Executrix and Trustee, I appoint _____, of _____ (city), _____ (province), to be my Executor/Executrix and Trustee.

2. I give my Executor/Executrix and Trustee all my property of every kind and wherever located to administer as I direct in this Will. My Executor/Executrix and Trustee shall be authorized to carry out all terms of this Will and pay my just debts, obligations and funeral expenses.

3. Bequests: After payment of my debts, I direct that my property be bequeathed as follows:

Page ___ of ____   Testator's Initials _____   Witness' Initials _____   Witness' Initials _____

4. Debts to be Paid From My Estate: Pay out of my estate the following:

5. Residue of Estate: I give the residue of my estate to   , if   survives me for 30 days; if   does not survive me for 30 days, to divide the residue of my estate into as many equal shares as I have children who survive me, except if any child of mine dies before me and leaves one or more of his or her children alive at my death, an equal share will also be created for that deceased child.

IN WITNESS WHEREOF I have signed my name to this and the preceding   pages at   (city),   (province), this   day of   , 2   .

_____
Testator's Signature

We were both present, at the request of

                    ,

when he/she signed this Will. We then signed as witnesses in his/her presence and in the presence of each other.

_____   _____
Signature of Witness   Signature of Witness

_____   _____
Printed Name   Printed Name

_____   _____
Address (Street)   Address (Street)

_____   _____
City   City

_____   _____
Province   Province

Page ___ of ___   _____   _____   _____
                    Testator's Initials   Witness' Initials   Witness' Initials

LEASE TERMINATION AGREEMENT

FOR GOOD CONSIDERATION, be it acknowledged that _____ of _____ (Lessee) and _____ of _____ (Lessor) under a certain lease agreement between the parties dated _____, 20____ (Lease), do hereby mutually agree to terminate and cancel said Lease effective _____, 20____. All rights and obligations under said Lease shall thereupon be cancelled excepting only for any rents under the Lease accruing prior to the effective termination date which then remain unpaid or otherwise not satisfied, and which shall be paid by Lessee on or prior to the termination date.

Lessee agrees to promptly surrender the premises to Lessor on or before the termination date and deliver same to Lessor in good condition free of the Lessee's goods and effects, waiving all further rights to possession.

This agreement shall be binding upon the parties, their successors, assigns and personal representatives.

Signed this _____ day of _____, 20____.

In the presence of:

_____   _____
Witness   Lessee

_____   _____
Witness   Lessor

LEAVE REQUEST / RETURN FROM LEAVE

Employee: _____ Date: _____

Position: _____ Date Hired: _____

<u>Leave Request</u>

Reason for Leave:

_____ Personal Disability

_____ Military

_____ Training Conference

_____ Compensatory Time Off

_____ Jury Duty

_____ Family Illness (Name)_____

_____ Family Death (Name) _____

_____ Other (Explain) _____

_____ _____

_____ _____

Leave Requested:

From: Date: _____ Time: _____ Total Hours: _____

To: Date: _____ Time: _____ Total Days: _____

Regular work schedule: _____

_____   _____
Employee   Date

<u>Return From Leave</u>

Absent From: Date: _____ Time: _____ Total Hours: _____

To: Date: _____ Time: _____ Total Days: _____

_____ Excused/Warranted

_____ Not Excused/Not Warranted (Explain) _____

_____ Resumed Part-Time Work

_____ Resumed Full-Time Work

_____ Resumed Modified Duty (Explain) _____

_____ Other (Explain) _____

Affirmed By:_____ Date:_____

LETTER OF COMMENDATION

Date:

To:

On behalf of our company, I am very pleased to commend you on your excellent job performance during this last review period from   to   .

Your efforts on behalf of the company are truly appreciated. Only through the devoted and tireless contributions of valued employees like yourself can we confidently look to the future.

Again, on behalf of the company and your co-employees, we salute you for a job well done.

                                                    Sincerely,

                                        _____

Copies to: Department/Personnel File

LETTER REQUESTING AUTHORIZATION TO RELEASE CREDIT INFORMATION

Thank you for your recent interest in establishing credit with our company. Please sign the authorization to release credit information below and complete the enclosed form. Then submit it to us with your most recent financial statements. We will contact your credit and bank references and then contact you regarding credit with our company.

Thank you,

Credit Manager

The undersigned has recently applied for credit with _____ .
The undersigned has been requested to provide information concerning my credit history. Therefore, I authorize the investigation of my credit information.

The release by you of information is authorized whether such information is of record or not. I do hereby release you and all persons, agencies, agents, employees, firms, companies, or parties affiliated with you from any damages resulting from providing such information.

This authorization is valid for thirty (30) days from the date of my signature below. Please keep a copy of my release request for your files.

Thank you for your cooperation.

Signature _____ Date _____

LIMITED GUARANTY

BE IT KNOWN, for good consideration, and as an inducement for

(Creditor) to extend credit from time to time to

(Customer), the undersigned jointly, severally and unconditionally guarantee to Creditor the prompt and punctual payment of certain sums now or hereinafter due Creditor from Customer, provided that the liability of the guarantors hereunder, whether singularly or collectively, shall be limited to the sum of $ as a maximum liability and guarantors shall not be liable under this guaranty for any greater or further amount.

The undersigned guarantors agree to remain fully bound on this guaranty, notwithstanding any extension, forbearance, indulgence or waiver, or release or discharge or substitution of any party or collateral or security for the debt. In the event of default, Creditor may seek payment directly from the undersigned without need to proceed first against borrower. Guarantors further waive all suretyship defenses consistent with this limited guaranty. In the event of default, the guarantor shall be responsible for all lawyer's fees and reasonable costs of collection, which may be in addition to the limited guaranty amount.

This guaranty shall be binding upon and inure to the benefit of the parties, their successors, assigns and personal representatives.

Signed this   day of   , 20   .

In the presence of:

_____   _____
Witness   Guarantor

_____   _____
Witness   Guarantor

LIST OF SHAREHOLDERS

I, _____, _____ Secretary of _____ Corporation, hereby certify the following list of shareholders who own all outstanding stock of the Corporation and who are entitled to vote at the shareholders' meeting on the _____ day of _____, 20___, because they were shareholders of record at the close of business on the _____ day of _____, 20___.

Total Number of Shares Owned	Total Number of Voting Shares Owned	Shareholder
_____	_____	_____
_____	_____	_____
_____	_____	_____
_____	_____	_____

Dated:

_____
Secretary of the Corporation

LOST CREDIT CARD NOTICE

Date:

To:

Dear

　　　　Please be advised that the below described credit card has been lost or stolen. You are therefore requested to stop issuance of further credit against said card until notified to the contrary by the undersigned.

　　　　Please notify me at once if charges appeared against said card after _____, 20____, as this was the date the card was lost or stolen and subsequent charges were unauthorized.

　　　　Please send me a replacement card.

　　　　Thank you for your cooperation.

Very truly yours,

_____
Cardholder

_____
Address

_____
Credit Card Number

REGISTERED MAIL

MAILING LIST NAME REMOVAL REQUEST

Date:

To:

Dear

    Please be advised that I have received unsolicited mail from your firm. I hereby request that you remove my name from your mailing list, and that you not send me unsolicited material in the future.

    My name and address appears as below (or as per mailing label attached).

Name

Street Address

City, Province

Thank you for your attention to this request.

                        Very truly yours,

MINUTES OF ANNUAL MEETING OF STOCKHOLDERS

_____

The annual meeting of stockholders of _____ was held at

_____ at

_____ .m., on _____ , 20 ___ .

The meeting was called to order by _____ , President, who chaired the meeting, and _____ , Secretary, kept the record of the meeting.

The Secretary stated that the following stockholders were present in person:

Names	Number of Shares
_____	_____
_____	_____
_____	_____
_____	_____

and that the following stockholders were represented by proxy:

Names	Number of Proxies	Number of Shares
_____	_____	_____
_____	_____	_____
_____	_____	_____
_____	_____	_____

The Chairman then reported that there were present in person and represented by proxy the number of shares necessary to constitute a quorum to conduct business.

The proxies presented were directed to be filed with the Secretary of the meeting.

The Chairman then stated that the next business to come before the meeting was the election of the Board of Directors to serve for the upcoming year.

The following were nominated as directors:

_____

_____

_____

No other persons were nominated.

Upon motion duly made, seconded and unanimously carried, the nominations were closed.

The ballots of the stockholders were presented and the Secretary reported that   ,   and   had received a plurality of the votes.

The Chairman then declared that the aforementioned persons were duly elected directors of the Corporation to hold office for the upcoming year.

No further business coming before the meeting, upon motion duly made, seconded and carried, the meeting adjourned.

_____
Secretary

MINUTES OF COMBINED MEETING OF STOCKHOLDERS AND DIRECTORS

A combined meeting of Stockholders and Directors was held at the office of the Corporation, at _____ on _____, 20___, at ___ .m.

The following Directors were present at the meeting:

_____ _____

_____ _____

_____ _____

being a quorum of the Directors of the Corporation.

The following Shareholders were present in person or by proxy at the meeting:

_____ _____

_____ _____

_____ _____

being a quorum of the Shareholders of the Corporation.

_____, President of the Corporation, chaired the meeting, and _____, Secretary of the Corporation, acted as secretary of the meeting.

The Secretary presented notice or waiver of notice of the meeting, signed by all interested parties.

The meeting, having been duly convened, was ready to proceed with its business, whereupon it was:

The Secretary announced that _____ shares of common stock had been voted in favor of the foregoing resolution(s) and _____ shares of common stock had been voted against the resolution(s), said vote representing more than _____% of the outstanding shares entitled to vote thereon.

The President thereupon declared that the resolution(s) had been duly adopted.

There being no further business, upon motion, the meeting was adjourned.

_____
Secretary

MINUTES OF DIRECTORS' MEETING

A regular meeting of the Board of Directors of   was duly called and held on   , 20   , at   commencing at   o'clock   .m.   There were present and participating at the meeting:

With approval of the directors present,   acted as Chair of the meeting and   recorded the minutes.

On motions duly made and seconded, it was voted that:

1. The minutes of the last meeting of directors be taken as read.

2. That it be further VOTED:

There being no further business, the meeting was adjourned.

Date:

_____
Secretary

MINUTES OF FIRST MEETING OF SHAREHOLDERS

The first meeting of the shareholders of   was held at   on the   day of   , 20   , at   o'clock   .m.

The meeting was duly called and held by order of the President. The President stated the purpose of the meeting.

Next, the Secretary read the list of shareholders as they appear in the record book of the Corporation, and noted that the required quorum of shareholders were present.

Next, the Secretary read a waiver of notice of the meeting, signed by all shareholders. On a motion duly made, seconded and carried, the waiver was ordered attached to the minutes of this meeting.

Next, the President asked the Secretary to read: (1) the minutes of the organization meeting of the Corporation, and (2) the minutes of the first meeting of the Board of Directors.

A motion was duly made, seconded and carried unanimously that the following resolution be adopted:

WHEREAS, the minutes of the organization meeting of the Corporation and the minutes of the first meeting of the Board of Directors have been read to this meeting, and

WHEREAS, bylaws were adopted and directors and officers were elected at the organization meeting, it is hereby

RESOLVED that this meeting approves and ratifies the election of the said directors and officers of this Corporation for the term of   years and approves, ratifies and adopts said bylaws as the bylaws of the corporation. It is further

RESOLVED that all acts taken and decisions made at the organization meeting and the first meeting of the Board are approved and ratified. It is further

RESOLVED that signing of these minutes constitutes full ratification by the signatories and waiver of notice of the meeting.

There being no further business, it was voted to adjourn the meeting, dated this day of _____, 20___.

_____
Secretary

_____

_____

_____

_____
Directors

Appended hereto:

    Waiver of notice of meeting

MINUTES OF SPECIAL MEETING OF STOCKHOLDERS

_____

A special meeting of the stockholders of the above Corporation was duly called and held at _____ , in the City of _____ , in the Province of _____ , on _____ , 20___ at _____ o'clock .___m.

The meeting was called to order by _____ , the President of the Corporation, and _____ , the Secretary of the Corporation, kept the records of the meeting and its proceedings.

The Secretary noted that a quorum of stockholders were present in person or were represented by proxy, the aggregate amount representing more than _____ % of the outstanding stock entitled to vote on the resolutions proposed at the meeting.

The Secretary reported that the following stockholders were present in person:

Names	Number of Shares
_____	_____
_____	_____
_____	_____

and that the following stockholders were represented by proxy:

Names	Names of Proxies	Number of Shares
_____	_____	_____
_____	_____	_____
_____	_____	_____

The Secretary presented and read a waiver of notice of the meeting signed by each stockholder entitled to notice of the meeting, said waiver of notice was ordered to be filed with the minutes of the meeting.

On motion duly made and seconded, and after due deliberation, the following resolution(s) was/were voted upon:

The Secretary reported that _____ shares of common stock had been voted in favor of the foregoing resolution(s) and _____ shares of common stock had been voted against the resolutions, said vote representing more than _____ % of the outstanding shares entitled to vote thereon.

The President thereupon declared that the resolution(s) had been duly adopted.

There being no further business, upon motion, the meeting adjourned.

A True Record

Attest

_____
Secretary

MUTUAL CANCELLATION OF CONTRACT

BE IT KNOWN, that for value received, that the undersigned
and _____ being parties to a certain contract dated _____, 20___, whereas said contract provides for:

do hereby mutually cancel and terminate said contract, effective this date.

We further provide that said termination shall be without further recourse by either party against the other and this document shall constitute mutual releases of any further obligations under said contract, all to the same extent as if said contract had not been entered into in the first instance, provided the parties shall herewith undertake the below described acts to terminate said contract, which obligations, if any, shall remain binding, notwithstanding this agreement to cancel.

Signed this _____ day of _____, 20___.

In the presence of:

_____   _____
Witness   First Party

_____   _____
Witness   Second Party

MUTUAL RELEASES

BE IT KNOWN, for good consideration, and in further consideration of the mutual releases herein entered into, that:

(First Party) and (Second Party) do hereby completely, mutually and reciprocally release, discharge, acquit and forgive each other from all claims, contracts, actions, suits, demands, agreements, liabilities, and proceedings of every nature and description both at law and in equity that either party has or may have against the other, arising from the beginning of time to the date of these presence, including but not necessarily limited to an incident or claim described as:

This release shall be binding upon and inure to the benefit of the parties, their successors, assigns and personal representatives.

Signed this   day of   , 20   .

In the presence of:

_____   _____
Witness   First Party

_____   _____
Witness   Second Party

NEW EMPLOYEE DATA

Name: _____

Employee Social Insurance No.: _____

Address: _____

Position: _____ Department: _____

Pay Frequency: _____ Pay Code: _____ Annual Salary: _____

Employment Date: _____ Employment Code: _____ Cost Center: _____

Sex: ❏ M   ❏ F

Marital Status:

❏ Single   ❏ Married   ❏ Separated   ❏ Widowed   ❏ Divorced

Birth Date: _____ Home Phone: _____

Driver's License No.: _____ Province: _____ Exp. Date: _____

Spouse's Name: _____

Children

Name: _____ Birth Date: _____

Name: _____ Birth Date: _____

Name: _____ Birth Date: _____

Name: _____ Birth Date: _____

Education

High School: _____ No. of Yrs.: _____ Degree: _____

University/College: _____ No. of Yrs.: _____ Degree: _____

Post-Graduate: _____ No. of Yrs.: _____ Degree: _____

Military Service: Branch_____ Rank _____ Discharge Date _____

Emergency Notification

Name: _____

Phone: _____ Relationship: _____

Address: _____

NO DECISION ON HIRING

Date:

To:

Dear

Thank you for your interest in employment with our company. You were among many well-qualified applicants who responded to our opening the position of

.

Unfortunately, we have decided not to fill the position at this time.

We will keep your resume on file for six months and will contact you should we decide to fill this position within that period.

Thank you and good luck in your job search.

Sincerely,

_____
Personnel Manager

NON-COMPETE AGREEMENT

FOR GOOD CONSIDERATION, the undersigned First Party jointly and severally covenant and agree not to compete with the business of
Second Party (Company), and its lawful successors and assigns.

The term "non compete" as used herein shall mean that the Undersigned shall not directly or indirectly engage in a business or other activity described as:

notwithstanding whether said participation be as an owner, officer, director, employee, agent, consultant, partner or stockholder (excepting as a passive investment in a publicly owned company).

This covenant shall extend only for a radius of _____ miles from the present location of the Company at _____ and shall remain in full force and effect for _____ years from date hereof.

In the event of any breach, the Company shall be entitled to full injunctive relief without need to post bond, which rights shall be cumulative with and not necessarily successive or exclusive of any other legal rights.

This agreement shall be binding upon and inure to the benefit of the parties, their successors, assigns and personal representatives.

Signed this _____ day of _____, 20___.

Witnessed:

_____   _____
Witness   First Party

_____   _____
Witness   Second Party

NON-DISCLOSURE OF TRADE SECRETS

In consideration of my being employed by
(Company), I the undersigned hereby agree and acknowledge the following:

1. That during my employment there may be disclosed to me certain trade secrets consisting of:

    a) Technical information: methods, processes, formulae, compositions, systems, techniques, inventions, machines, computer programs and research projects.

    b) Business information: customer lists, pricing data, sources of supply, and marketing, production, or merchandising systems or plans.

2. I agree that during and after the termination of my employment, I shall not use for myself or others, or disclose or divulge to others, any trade secrets, confidential information, or any other data of the Company in violation of this agreement.

3. Upon terminating my employment with the Company:

    a) I shall return to the Company all documents and property pertaining to the Company, including but not limited to: drawings, blueprints, records, reports, manuals, correspondence, customer lists, computer programs, inventions, and all other materials and all copies thereof relating in any way to the Company's business and in any way obtained by me during my employment. I further agree that I shall not retain any copies or reproductions of the foregoing.

    b) The Company may notify any future or prospective employer of this agreement.

    c) This agreement shall be binding upon me and my personal representatives and successors in interest, and shall inure to the benefit of the Company, its successors and assigns.

    d) The enforceability of any one provision to this agreement shall not impair or affect any other terms of this agreement.

    e) In the event of any breach of this agreement, the Company shall have full rights to injunctive relief, in addition to any other existing rights, without requirement of posting bond, if permitted by law.

_____   _____
Employee   Date

_____
Company

_____   _____
By   Date

NOTICE OF 30-DAY EVALUATION

Date:

To:

    As a result of your failure to correct the problem described below, even after oral discussions and a written warning, you are now being placed on a 30-day formal evaluation, effective _____ , 20____.

As we discussed earlier, the problem with your performance is:

The targets we agreed upon for your period of evaluation are:

    I have scheduled a counseling session on _____ , 20____ , to meet with you and go over your progress during this period. Please be assured that I will be available for discussions and counseling at any time during this evaluation. I truly hope this action will result in positive improvement. Failure to correct this situation, however, will result in your termination, either at the end of the evaluation period, or before that time if no improvement is evident.

_____   _____
Supervisor   Date

_____   _____
Supervisor's Manager   Date

_____   _____
Personnel Manager   Date

NOTICE OF ANNUAL SHAREHOLDERS' MEETING

Notice is hereby given that the annual meeting of shareholders of _____ shall be held on _____, 20___, at _____.m., in the offices of the Corporation at _____, in the City of _____.

The shareholders will deliberate and take action on the following matters:

1. The election of a new Board of Directors for the year beginning _____, 20___, and ending _____, 20___.

2. Transact such other business as may properly come before the meeting or any adjournment thereof.

Only those shareholders who were shareholders of record at the close of business on _____, 20___, will be entitled to vote in person or by proxy at the meeting or any adjournment thereof.

By order of the Board of Directors

of _____ Corporation

_____
Secretary

Dated:

NOTICE OF ASSIGNMENT

Date:

To:

Dear

    You are hereby notified that on _____, 20____, we have assigned and transferred to _____ the following _____ existing between us:

    Please direct any further correspondence (or payments, if applicable) to them at the following address:

_____

_____

_____

    Please contact us should you have any questions, and we thank you for your cooperation.

    Very truly yours,

_____

NOTICE OF ASSIGNMENT TO OBLIGOR

Date:

To:

Dear

      Please take notice of the attached assignment, and hold all sums of money affected by such assignment, now or hereafter in your possession, that otherwise are payable to me, for the benefit of _____, Assignee, in accordance with the provisions of said assignment, and the terms of our original agreement.

      An authenticated copy of this assignment was filed by me on _____, 20____, in the office of the _____.

                                      Very truly yours,

                                      _____

NOTICE OF AVAILABLE POSITION

Starting Date: _____ Date Posted: _____

Position: _____

Description Of Duties:

Qualifications Required:

Salary:

Contact:

NOTICE OF C.O.D. TERMS

Date:

To:

Dear

    We are in receipt of your order dated _____, 20___, and your request for credit terms.

    While we do want to accept your order, we regret we cannot ship on credit terms at the present time, due to inadequate credit.

    Accordingly, we propose shipment on C.O.D. terms. We will assume C.O.D. terms are satisfactory to you unless we are notified of the contrary within ten (10) days.

    Thank you for your understanding and we appreciate your patronage, with the hope we may more favorably consider credit requests in the future.

    Very truly yours,

_____

NOTICE OF CASH-ONLY TERMS

Date:

To:

Dishonored cheques create severe accounting problems for us even if they are subsequently paid, and impose bank charges that we must charge back to the customer.

Your record of dishonored C.O.D. cheques has prompted us to restrict future shipments to you to a cash-on-delivery basis. Bank or certified cheques, however, are allowed. You may contact us prior to shipment for the exact order amount so you will be prepared to accept delivery on the terms stated above. We regret this action is necessary, but we are confident you understand our position.

We apologize for any inconvenience this may cause you, but look forward to your continued patronage.

Very truly,

_____

NOTICE OF CHANGE IN RENT

Date:

To:

Dear

     Please be advised that effective   , 20   , the monthly rent for the rented premises you now occupy as my Tenant at   shall be increased to $ per month, payable in advance on the   day of each month during your continued tenancy. This is a change from your present rent of $ per month.

     All other terms of your tenancy shall remain as presently in effect.

                                          Very truly yours,

                                          _____

                                          Landlord

NOTICE OF CONFIDENTIALITY AGREEMENT

Date:

To:

Re:

It has come to our attention that the above-named individual, whom we previously employed, is now employed by your organization.

We wish to notify you of certain continuing obligations that said individual has to our company concerning confidential trade secrets and other proprietary information that may have been acquired or developed during this individual's employ with our company.

It is not our intention to prevent this individual, nor any other former employee, from using the general knowledge of the industry or skills acquired while employed by our company. Protecting our company's confidential information is our only concern. As a business organization also possessing confidential data and trade secrets, you can appreciate our position, I am sure. Your cooperation in this matter will be greatly appreciated.

For informational purposes, I am also sending a copy of this letter to:

Sincerely,

_____

NOTICE OF CORRECTED ACCOUNT

Date:

To:

Thank you for bringing to our attention the error in your statement.

We have thoroughly checked our records and find that you were correct. Therefore, we shall immediately issue a credit to your account which shall appear on your next statement.

Please accept our apology for any inconvenience this error may have caused you.

Very truly,

_____

NOTICE OF DEBT ASSIGNMENT

Date:

To:

Re: Balance Due To:

Dear

Reference is made to a certain debt or obligation due from you to the above referenced party.

On _____, 20___, all rights to receive future payment have been assigned to the undersigned. A copy of the assignment is attached. We understand the balance due is $ _____.

Accordingly, we provide you notice of said assignment and direct that all future payments on said account be directed to the undersigned at the below address. Further, cheques should be made payable to the undersigned.

It is important that all payments be made as directed to ensure credit. You understand this is not a dunning notice or a reflection on your credit.

We appreciate your cooperation.

Very truly yours,

_____
Signature of Assignee

_____
Name of Assignee

_____
Address of Assignee

_____

NOTICE OF DEFAULT IN PAYMENT

Date:

To:

You are hereby notified that your payment of Dollars ($) due on or before   , has not been received by the undersigned. If said payment is not paid by   , the undersigned shall invoke the remedies under the agreement between us dated   , together with such other remedies that the undersigned may have.

NOTICE OF DEFAULT ON EXTENSION AGREEMENT

Date:

To:

Your payment, due _____, 20____, in accordance with an extension agreement, has not been received. The agreement terms specify that you make weekly/monthly payments of $_____ each.

If this lack of payment was due to oversight, please pay within the next five (5) days, and we shall be pleased to honor the extended terms.

If the requested payment is not made, we shall have no choice but to immediately enforce our rights to void the extension agreement and collect the present balance of $_____.

We hope you shall make payment and avoid any added expense of collection as provided for in the agreement.

Very truly,

_____

NOTICE OF DEFAULT ON PROMISSORY NOTE

Date:

To:

Dear

    We refer to your promissory note dated _____, 20___, in the original principal amount of $ _____ and to which we, the undersigned, are holder.

    Notice is hereby provided that you are in default under said note in that the following payment(s) have not been received.

    <u>Payment Due Date</u>   <u>Amount Due</u>

                        Total Arrears $ _____

    Accordingly, demand is hereby made for full payment of the entire balance of $ _____ due under the note. If payment is not received within _____ days, this note shall be forwarded to our lawyers for collection and you shall additionally be liable for all reasonable cost of collection, and accrued interest and late charges.

                                      Very truly yours,

                                      _____

NOTICE OF DISMISSAL

Date:

To:

    We regret to notify you that your employment with the firm shall be terminated on _____, 20____, for the following reasons:

    Severance pay shall be in accordance with company policy. We shall also issue to you a statement of accrued benefits. Insurance benefits shall continue according to applicable law and/or the provisions of our employee policy. Please contact _____ at your earliest convenience, who will arrange other termination matters with you.

    We truly regret this action is necessary.

                                              Sincerely,

                                            _____

Copies to:

NOTICE OF DISPUTED ACCOUNT

Date:

To:

Dear   :

We refer to your Invoice or Statement No.   , dated   , 20   , in the amount of $.

We dispute the balance claimed for the following reason(s):

_____ Items billed for have not been received.

_____ Prices are in excess of agreed amount. Credit of $ is claimed.

_____ Prior payment made in the amount of $ made on   , 20   , was not credited.

_____ Goods were unordered, and are available for return on shipping instructions.

_____ Goods were defective as per prior notice.

_____ Goods are available for return and credit per sales items.

_____ Other:

Therefore, we request you promptly credit our account in the amount of $ so that this account may be satisfactorily cleared.

Very truly yours,

_____

NOTICE OF ELECTION TO CANCEL

Date:

To:

    You are hereby notified that _____ has elected to cancel and terminate, and cancels and terminates, effective _____, 20___, the following written contract entered into with you, all in accordance with the terms and provisions of the contract:

                                                         _____

NOTICE OF FORFEITURE

Date:

To:

Please take notice that the undersigned elects to declare the agreement forfeited and void that was executed by you and the undersigned on _____, 20___, for the reason that you have failed to abide by the terms of the agreement in the following manner:

_____

NOTICE OF INTENT TO REPOSSESS DUE TO DEFAULT

Date:

To:

You are in default under a certain lease contract dated _____ for the following reason(s):

This letter serves as notice to you of said default. It is also notice to you that, unless you communicate with the undersigned within _____ days from the date of this letter, we shall exercise our rights upon default as stated in the lease contract, including our right to take immediate possession of the following leased item(s):

Very truly yours,

_____

NOTICE OF PROBATION

Date:

To:

You have received earlier warnings of unsatisfactory performance or violation of our personnel rules.

As you can understand, we do everything possible to retain good employees. When repeated violations or poor performance continues, we usually have no other choice but to dismiss the employee.

However, we do want to give you one final opportunity to prove your value to our company. With that objective we are placing you on a   -month probation. If there is continued unsatisfactory performance during this probationary period, we shall have no alternative but to terminate your employment.

Please accept this as a chance to prove to both yourself and us that our confidence in you was justified.

Please contact   upon receipt of this notice, as we do want to review your employment record with you, clarify the conditions of probation and assist you in whatever way possible toward improved performance.

Sincerely,

_____

Copies to:

NOTICE OF RENT ARREARS

Date:

To:

You are hereby notified that your monthly rental payment of _____ Dollars ($ _____) was due on or before _____, and it has not been received to date. If said sum is not paid by _____, I shall invoke the remedies made available to me under Section _____ of a certain lease agreement between us dated _____, relating to failure to pay the agreed rent.

_____

NOTICE OF RESULTS OF PUBLIC SALE

Date:

To:

    Please take notice that on _____, 20____, the public resale of goods which had been identified in a certain agreement dated _____, 20____, consisting of _____, was held in accordance with the notice sent to you on _____, 20____.

    Said goods were resold at auction for $_____, which was less than our agreed price of $_____. Accordingly, I am holding you liable for said amount, together with incidental expenses of $_____.

    If you do not remit the total amount of $_____ within ____ days, I shall refer the matter to my lawyer for collection.

                                               Very truly yours,

                                             _____

NOTICE OF TERMINATION
DUE TO ABSENCE

Date:

To:

    We regret to inform you that your employment with the company shall terminate on _____, 20___, due to repeated non-authorized absences.

    We previously warned you about unauthorized absences in violation of company policy. However, your record shows repeated absences. A copy of your employment attendance record is available for your review.

    Severance pay shall be in accordance with company policy. We shall issue to you a statement of accrued benefits. Insurance benefits shall continue in accordance with applicable law and/or the provisions of our employee policy.

    Please contact _____ at your earliest convenience, who will arrange other termination matters with you.

    We truly regret this action is necessary.

                                 Sincerely,

                               _____

Copies to:

NOTICE OF TERMINATION
DUE TO WORK RULES VIOLATION

Date:

To:

You are hereby given notice that your employment with the company shall be terminated on _____, 20___.

This action is necessary due to the following violations of company work rules:

Your final paycheque shall be for the period ending _____, 20___. There shall be no severance pay since your termination was for just cause.

Please contact _____ concerning insurance coverage or other accrued benefits to which you may be entitled.

We regret this action is necessary and wish you success in your future endeavors.

Sincerely,

_____

NOTICE OF UNPAID INVOICE

Date:

To:

Dear

On _____, 20___, we received your cheque for $_____ representing payment on the following invoice(s):

        Invoice(s)   Amount

However, this did not include payment on the following overdue invoice(s) which remain unpaid, and are now overdue.

        Invoice(s)   Amount

In reviewing your account we assume the unpaid invoice(s) are due to oversight. Please advise if you need copies of the unpaid invoice(s) or if there is a question regarding the invoice(s). Otherwise, we shall anticipate prompt payment on these outstanding invoice(s). The total balance due is $_____.

We look forward to your prompt attention to this matter.

                                        Very truly yours,

                                        _____

NOTICE OF WAIVER OF
ANNUAL MEETING BY ALL SHAREHOLDERS

We, the undersigned, being the holders of all of the outstanding shares of stock of _____, do hereby waive notice of the annual meeting of shareholders scheduled to be held in the office of the Corporation at _____, in the City of _____, on _____, 20___, at ___.m.

The undersigned understand that the purposes of the meeting are to:

(1) Elect a new board of directors.

(2) Conduct any other business that properly may be brought before the meeting.

Shareholder	Date	Number of Shares
_____	_____	_____
_____	_____	_____
_____	_____	_____

NOTICE OF WRONGFUL REFUSAL TO ACCEPT DELIVERY

Date:

To:

    Reference is made to your order dated _____, 20___, a copy of which is attached.

    We have shipped said order in accordance with its terms but you have refused to accept delivery of said goods, and therefore we consider the purchase contract to have been wrongfully terminated by you.

    Accordingly, we shall not attempt further shipment, and shall hold you liable for all damages arising from your failure to fulfill your obligations under the order.

    Should you wish to rectify the situation by now accepting shipment, then you must call us immediately, and we shall arrange re-shipment at your expense.

    Should you have any questions on this matter, then please notify us immediately.

                                              Very truly yours,

                                        _____

NOTICE TO CANCEL BACK-ORDERED GOODS

Date:

To:

Dear

    Reference is made to our purchase order dated   , 20   , a copy of which is attached.

    We have received a partial shipment and notice that certain goods on said order are out of stock or on back order.

    Please cancel our order for the back-ordered goods and adjust our invoice accordingly to reflect only the goods received. If the back-ordered goods are in transit to us, please advise us at once, and we shall issue further instructions.

                                      Very truly yours,

                                      _____

NOTICE TO CANCEL DELAYED GOODS

Date:

To:

Dear

Reference is made to our purchase order or contract dated   , 20   , a copy of which is attached.

Under the terms of said order, the goods were to be shipped by   , 20   , or such further reasonable time as allowed by law.

Due to your failure to ship the goods within the time required, we hereby cancel said order, reserving such further rights and remedies as we may have, including damage claims under applicable law.

If said goods are in transit, they shall be refused or returned at your expense, and we shall await shipping instructions.

Very truly yours,

_____

NOTICE TO CREDITOR TO PAY SPECIFIC ACCOUNTS

Date:

To:

The enclosed cheque numbered   , in the amount of $,
dated   , 20   and drawn on
                         bank, is to be applied towards outstanding balances on the
following invoiced accounts only:

Invoice No.   Date of Invoice   Name of Creditor   Date Payment Due   Amount to be Credited

Please be certain the above amounts are credited to the proper accounts.

Sincerely yours,

NOTICE TO DIRECTORS OF SPECIAL MEETING

Date:

    A special meeting of the Board of Directors of _____ will be held on _____, 20___, at _____ .m., in the offices of the Corporation located at _____, in the City of _____, and Province of _____ to deliberate the following matter:

_____
Secretary

NOTICE TO EXERCISE LEASE OPTION

Date:

To:

Dear

    Reference is made to a certain lease between us dated   , 20 , for premises at   .

    Under the terms of said lease we have the option to extend or renew said lease for a term of   years commencing on   , 20 .

    This notice is provided to advise you of our intention to exercise the option to so renew or extend the lease on the terms therein contained.

                                                                                       Lessee (Tenant)

Registered Mail

NOTICE TO LANDLORD TO MAKE REPAIRS

Date:

To:

You are hereby notified to make the following repairs:

on the premises at:

I request you to make such repairs and to do all other acts necessary to put the premises in good repair pursuant to the provisions contained in a certain lease between us dated .

_____

NOTICE TO OFFICER OF REMOVAL FROM BOARD

Date:

To:

PLEASE TAKE NOTICE that, pursuant to Article   , Section   of the Bylaws of this Corporation, the Board of Directors did, at a meeting held on   , 20   , adopt a resolution removing you forthwith from the Office of the Director, a copy of which resolution is annexed hereto and the original of which is on file in the principal office of the Corporation.

                                                                               Secretary

NOTICE TO PURCHASER OF BREACH OF OPTION

Date:

To:

      Please take notice that, as you have   , in violation of the provisions of a certain option, dated   , to purchase real property and by which you hold possession of that property, the option, and all rights, title, and interest under said option, is hereby terminated and you are given   days from receipt of this notice to surrender possession to the undersigned.

                                                  _____

NOTICE TO RECLAIM GOODS

Date:

To:

Dear

Reference is made to certain goods that have been shipped and received by you within the past ten (10) days as represented by the attached invoices.

It has come to our attention that your firm is insolvent, and therefore we demand return and reclamation of all goods delivered to you within the ten (10) days preceding this notice.

In the event any of the aforesaid goods have been sold, this shall constitute a priority claim for the value of said goods not available for return, and demand is made for the return of the balance of said goods within your possession.

Please advise as to shipping arrangements.

Very truly yours,

_____

NOTICE TO REDIRECT PAYMENTS

Date:

To:

      You are hereby notified that effective   , 20   , the party to whom payments should be made pursuant to our agreement dated   , 20   , is   , at the following address:

_____

NOTICE TO RE-ISSUE CHEQUE

Date:

To:

On   , 20   , you told us that you mailed your cheque in the amount of $.

Unfortunately, we have not yet received your cheque. We therefore suggest you notify your bank to stop payment on that cheque, and immediately issue to us a replacement cheque.

Enclosed please find a self-addressed envelope. This will help avoid any postal error. Thank you for your prompt cooperation in this matter.

Very truly,

_____

NOTICE TO REMEDY DEFAULT BY TENANT

Date:

To:

    Take notice that you have failed to _____, which you are required to do pursuant to clause _____ of the lease under which you occupy the premises located at: _____. You are further notified that if you fail to comply with said clause within _____ days of receipt of this notice, the undersigned will proceed to terminate this lease according to the terms of said lease.

_____

NOTICE TO SHAREHOLDERS
OF ANNUAL MEETING

Notice is hereby given that the Annual Meeting of Shareholders of   shall be held for the purpose of electing a Board of Directors for the ensuing year and transacting such other business as may properly come before the board. The meeting, will be held on the   day of   , 20   , at   .m., at   , City of   , and Province of   .

Transfer books will remain closed from the   day of   , 20   , until the   day of   , 20   .

Dated the   day of   , 20

By Order of the Board of Directors

_____
Secretary

NOTICE TO STOP CREDIT CHARGE

Date:

To:

Dear   :

    Please be advised that on   , 20   , the undersigned charged the sum of $ on a transaction with   (Company).

    We hereby instruct you not to honor said charge or issue payment to the company for the following reason:

Thank you for your cooperation.

_____
Cardholder

_____
Address

_____

_____
Credit Card Number

REGISTERED MAIL

NOTICE TO STOP GOODS IN TRANSIT

Date:

To:

Dear   :

You are in receipt of certain goods in transit shipped by us and scheduled for delivery to the following consignee:

A copy of our shipping documents is enclosed.

You are hereby instructed to stop transit of said goods, not to make delivery to the consignee and to return said goods to us. We shall pay return freight charges.

No negotiable bill of lading or document of title has been delivered to our customer (consignee).

Very truly yours,

_____

Copy to:

_____
Customer

NOTICE TO TENANT TO MAKE REPAIRS

Date:

To:

You are hereby notified that the repairs specified in the attached schedule, marked as Exhibit A, are required to be made to the premises now occupied by you located at:

and I request you to make such repairs and to do all other acts necessary to put the premises in good repair pursuant to your responsibilities as contained in your lease for the said premises dated   , 20   .

_____

OPTION TO PURCHASE

OPTION AGREEMENT by and between   (Owner) and   (Buyer).

1.   Buyer hereby pays to Owner the sum of $ in consideration for this option, which option payment shall be credited to the purchase price if the option is exercised.

2.   Buyer has the option and right to buy   (property) within the option period for the full price of $.

3.   This option shall remain in effect until   , 20   , and thereupon expire unless this option is sooner exercised.

4.   To exercise this option, Buyer must notify Owner of same by registered mail within the option period. All notices shall be sent to owner at the following address:

5.   Should the Buyer exercise the option, the Owner and Buyer agree to promptly sign the attached contract of sale, and consummate the sale on its terms, which are incorporated herein by reference.

6.   This option agreement shall be binding upon and inure to the benefit of the parties, their successors, assigns and personal representatives.

Signed this   day of   , 20   .

_____   _____
Signature of Owner   Signature of Buyer

_____   _____
Name of Owner   Name of Buyer

_____   _____
Address of Owner   Address of Buyer

OPTION TO PURCHASE STOCK

     In consideration of   Dollars ($), the receipt of which is hereby acknowledged, the undersigned,   , hereby gives to   , for a period of   days from the date hereof, the right to purchase   shares of the stock of   at the price of   Dollars ($) per share. This option can be exercised only by the payment of cash before its expiration.

Date:

                                                        _____

PARTIAL SHIPMENT REQUEST

Date:

To:

Dear

    Thank you for your order dated _____, 20____. The amount of the order is approximately $_____. However, we regret we cannot extend credit to you for the entire amount at the present time.

    Accordingly, we suggest we ship you on our standard credit terms a partial order reducing quantities by _____ percent. Upon payment we shall release the balance of the order. If you request a different order configuration we would, of course, be pleased to accommodate you.

    Unless we hear from you to the contrary within the next ten (10) days, we shall assume you accept our recommendation, and we shall ship accordingly.

    Hopefully, we shall soon be in a position to increase your credit line.

                                               Very truly yours,

                                           _____

PAST DUE REMINDER

Date:

To:

Dear

    Please take note that your account is past due in the amount of Dollars ($). We sent you a statement a short time ago.

    Please remit payment to us as soon as possible.

                                      Thank you,

                                  _____

PAYMENT INQUIRY

Date:

To:

Dear

 We are at a loss to understand why your account balance of $ has not been paid.

 Perhaps you can now take a moment and help resolve it. Please complete the below portion and return it to us.

_____ The account has not been paid because:

_____ The account will be paid on or before   , 20 .

_____ Our cheque is enclosed. Sorry for the delay.

Thank you for your prompt consideration.

            Very truly yours,

            _____

PAYMENT ON SPECIFIC ACCOUNTS

Date:

To:

Dear

    We enclose our Cheque No. _____ in the amount of $ _____ . This cheque is to be credited to the following charges or invoices only:

Invoice/Debt	Amount
_____	$_____
_____	$_____
_____	$_____
_____	$_____
_____	$_____

You understand that payment herein shall be applied only to the specific items listed and shall not be applied, in whole or in part, to any other obligation, charge or invoice that may be outstanding.

                                        Very truly yours,

                                        _____

PAYMENT ON WRITTEN INSTRUMENT

Date:

      Received this day from   the sum of   Dollars ($) on account of the payments referred to in the note given by the above to me and dated   , 20   .

                                                    _____

PAYMENTS TO A CREDITOR
(use a separate form for each creditor)

Creditor:

Address:

Telephone/Fax:

Balance owed: $

Amount agreed to be paid: $

How to be paid:

Record of Payments

Date	Amount Paid	Balance
_____	$ _____	$ _____
_____	$ _____	$ _____
_____	$ _____	$ _____
_____	$ _____	$ _____
_____	$ _____	$ _____
_____	$ _____	$ _____
_____	$ _____	$ _____
_____	$ _____	$ _____
_____	$ _____	$ _____
_____	$ _____	$ _____
_____	$ _____	$ _____
_____	$ _____	$ _____
_____	$ _____	$ _____
_____	$ _____	$ _____
_____	$ _____	$ _____
_____	$ _____	$ _____

PERMISSION TO USE COPYRIGHTED MATERIAL

FOR GOOD CONSIDERATION, and in consideration of the sum of $ to be paid herewith, the undersigned, as copyright holder, hereby grants permission to _____ to reprint, publish and use for world distribution the following material:

This material shall be used only in the following manner or publication:

A credit line to acknowledge use of the material is/is not required. If required, the credit line shall read as follows:

This agreement shall be binding upon and inure to the benefit of the parties, their successors, assigns and personal representatives.

Signed this _____ day of _____, 20____.

In the presence of:

_____   _____
Witness   Name

PERMISSION TO USE QUOTE OR PERSONAL STATEMENT

FOR GOOD CONSIDERATION, the Undersigned irrevocably authorizes _____ and its successors and assigns the worldwide rights to use, publish or reprint in whole or in part, the following statement, picture, endorsement, quotation or other material:

This authorization shall extend only to a certain publication known as _____, including all new editions, reprints, excerpts, advertisements, publicity and promotions thereto of said work, and further including such publications as hold subsidiary rights thereto.

The Undersigned acknowledges that the permission granted herein is non-revocable, and that no further payment is due therein.

This agreement shall be binding upon and inure to the benefit of the parties, their successors, assigns and personal representatives.

Signed this _____ day of _____, 20____.

Witnessed:

_____ _____
Witness   Name

_____ _____
Witness   Address

                                  _____
                                  City, Province, Postal Code

PERSONAL PROPERTY RENTAL AGREEMENT

AGREEMENT made between _____ (Owner) and _____ (Renter):

1. Owner hereby rents to renter the below described personal property:

2. Renter shall pay to Owner the sum of $_____ as payment for the rental herein, said sum payable as follows:

3. The Renter shall during the rental term keep and maintain the property in good condition and repair and shall be responsible for any loss, casualty, damage or destruction to said property notwithstanding how caused, and Renter agrees to return said property in its present condition, reasonable wear and tear excepted.

4. The Renter shall not during the rental period allow others the use of the property.

5. The rental period shall commence on _____, 20___, and terminate on _____, 20___, at which date the property shall be promptly returned.

6. Other terms:

Signed this _____ day of _____, 20___.

In the presence of:

_____ _____
Witness   Owner

                              _____
                              Renter

PERSONNEL DATA CHANGE

Employee: _____ Employment Date: _____

Department: _____ Supervisor: _____

Effective Date: _____ Social Insurance No.: _____

Change/Update Employee Personnel File as Follows:

Name (Marital) Change: _____

New Address: _____

New Telephone No.: _____

Marital Status: _____

Number of Dependents: _____

Number of Exemptions: _____

Other:

_____   _____
Employee   Date

_____   _____
Supervisor   Date

PERSONNEL DATA SHEET

Employee: _____

Employment Date: _____ Social Insurance No.: _____

Address: _____

_____ Phone: _____

New Address: _____

_____ Phone: _____

Emergency Contact: _____ Phone: _____

Marital Status: _____ Spouse Name: _____

Type of Personnel Change	Date	Pay Increase	Merit/Promotion/Other
_____	_____	_____	_____
_____	_____	_____	_____
_____	_____	_____	_____
_____	_____	_____	_____
_____	_____	_____	_____
_____	_____	_____	_____
_____	_____	_____	_____
_____	_____	_____	_____
_____	_____	_____	_____
_____	_____	_____	_____
_____	_____	_____	_____
_____	_____	_____	_____
_____	_____	_____	_____
_____	_____	_____	_____
_____	_____	_____	_____

PRELIMINARY EMPLOYMENT APPLICATION

I understand that this is not a full application. I understand this application will be reviewed and my qualifications considered for possible job openings in the future.

Name: _____ Date: _____

Address: _____ City: _____

Province: _____ Postal Code: _____ Phone: _____

Position Desired: _____ Requested Wages: $_____ per _____

TYPE OF EMPLOYMENT

☐ Seasonal   ☐ Temporary   ☐ Permanent   ☐ Full Time   ☐ Part Time

Days available: ☐ Monday through Friday   ☐ Other (explain) _____

_____ Hours available: _____ to _____

EMPLOYMENT

Most Recent or Previous Employer: _____

Dates Employed: _____ to: _____ Wages: $ _____ per _____

Describe Position & Duties: _____

EDUCATION

Enter the number of years completed:

High School: _____   University/College: _____   Graduate/Professional School: _____

Describe your major area(s) of study: _____

_____

Other training: _____

List other relevent information: _____

_____

All potential employees are evaluated without regard to race, color, religion, gender, national origin, age, marital or veteran status, the presence of a non-job related handicap or any other legally protected status.

Signature: _____ Date: _____

Print Name: _____

PRESENTMENT BY MAIL

Date:

To:

The undersigned,   of   , is the holder of a certain instrument, dated   , 20   , made by you for the payment of   Dollars ($) on   , 20   , to the order of   of   . The undersigned, being the present holder of said instrument, hereby demands payment of this note.

_____

PRIVACY RELEASE

Agreement made this _____ day of _____, 20___, that in consideration of _____ Dollars ($_____), receipt of which is acknowledged, I, _____, do hereby grant _____ and his or her assigns, licensees, and legal representatives the irrevocable right to use my name (or any fictional name), picture, portrait, or photograph in all forms and media in all manners, including composite or distorted representations, for advertising, trade, or any other lawful purposes, and I waive any right to inspect or approve the finished version(s), including written copy that may be created in connection therewith. I am of lawful age.* I have read this release and am fully familiar with its contents.

_____ _____
Witness   Grantor

_____ _____
Address   Address

Consent (if applicable)

I am the parent or guardian of the minor named above and have the legal authority to execute the above release. I approve the foregoing and consent to same on behalf of said minor.

_____ _____
Witness   Parent or Guardian

_____ _____
Address   Address

Date:

* Delete this sentence if the subject is a minor. The parent or guardian must then sign the consent section.

PRODUCT DEFECT CLAIM

Date:

To:

Dear

    We have sold to a customer a product sold or manufactured by you named and described as:

    We have been advised by the customer of a product defect or warranty claim in the following particulars:

        Name of Customer:

        Date of Purchase:

        Claimed Defect:

        Injuries or Damage Claimed:

    In the event suit or claim is brought against us arising from breach of warranty of merchantability, or any such similar claim arising from said product, we shall in a like manner look to you for full reimbursement and indemnification.

    This letter is provided to give you earliest possible notice of a potential claim, and to preserve our rights against you should such a claim arise.

    We shall advise you upon receipt of any further information on this claim.

                Very truly yours,

_____

PRODUCT DEFECT NOTICE

Date:

To:

Dear

Notice is hereby provided that we have purchased a product manufactured, distributed or sold by you and described as:

You are advised of a product defect or warranty claim. In support of same we provide the following information:

1. DATE OF PURCHASE:

2. NATURE OF DEFECT:

3. INJURIES OR DAMAGE:

4. ITEM PURCHASED FROM:

This is provided to give you earliest possible notice of said claim. I request that you or your representative contact me as soon as possible.

Very truly yours,

_____
Name

_____
Address

_____
City, Province, Postal Code

_____
Telephone Number

REGISTERED MAIL

PRODUCT WARRANTY CLAIM

Date:

To:

Dear

    Please be advised that we purchased the following named product, _____ ,

from _____ , on _____ , 20____ .

    This product is defective or in need of repair in the following particulars:

    This product is under a full warranty and we therefore request repair of the product under the warranty terms.

    Accordingly:

        _____ Product is enclosed for repair/replacement and return.

        _____ Please call (_____) for a service appointment.

Thank you for your cooperation in this matter.

                              Very truly yours,

_____

Name

_____

Address

_____

City, Province, Postal Code

_____

Telephone

PROMISSORY NOTE

Principal amount $ Date:

    FOR VALUE RECEIVED, the undersigned hereby jointly and severally promise to pay to the order of   the sum of   Dollars ($), together with interest thereon at the rate of   % per annum on the unpaid balance. Said sum shall be paid in the manner following:

    All payments shall be first applied to interest and the balance to principal. This note may be prepaid, at any time, in whole or in part, without penalty.

    This note shall at the option of any holder thereof be immediately due and payable upon the occurrence of any of the following: 1) Failure to make any payment due hereunder within   days of its due date. 2) Breach of any condition of any security interest, mortgage, loan agreement, pledge agreement or guarantee granted as collateral security for this note. 3) Breach of any condition of any loan agreement, security agreement or mortgage, if any, having a priority over any loan agreement, security agreement or mortgage on collateral granted, in whole or in part, as collateral security for this note. 4) Upon the death, incapacity, dissolution or liquidation of any of the undersigned, or any endorser, guarantor to surety hereto. 5) Upon the filing by any of the undersigned of an assignment for the benefit of creditors, bankruptcy or other form of insolvency, or by suffering an involuntary petition in bankruptcy or receivership not vacated within thirty (30) days.

    In the event this note shall be in default and placed for collection, then the undersigned agree to pay all reasonable lawyers' fees and costs of collection. Payments not made within five (5) days of due date shall be subject to a late charge of   % of said payment. All payments hereunder shall be made to such address as may from time to time be designated by any holder.

The undersigned and all other parties to this note, whether as endorsers, guarantors or sureties, agree to remain fully bound until this note shall be fully paid and waive demand, presentment and protest and all notices hereto, and further agree to remain bound, notwithstanding any extension, modification, waiver, or other indulgence or discharge or release of any obligor hereunder, or exchange, substitution, or release of any collateral granted as security for this note. No modification or indulgence by any holder hereof shall be binding unless in writing, and any indulgence on any one occasion shall not be an indulgence for any other or future occasion. Any modification or change in terms, hereunder granted by any holder hereof, shall be valid and binding upon each of the undersigned, notwithstanding the acknowledgement of any of the undersigned, and each of the undersigned does hereby irrevocably grant to each of the others a power of attorney to enter into any such modification on their behalf. The rights of any holder hereof shall be cumulative and not necessarily successive. This note shall take effect as a sealed instrument and shall be construed, governed and enforced in accordance with the laws of the Province of   .

Witnessed:

_____   _____
Witness   Borrower

_____   _____
Witness   Borrower

GUARANTY

We the undersigned jointly and severally guaranty the prompt and punctual payment of all moneys due under the aforesaid note and agree to remain bound until fully paid.

In the presence of:

_____   _____
Witness   Guarantor

_____   _____
Witness   Guarantor

PROPOSAL TO BUY A BUSINESS

Date:

To:

Re: Purchase of

    The undersigned is interested in negotiating an agreement for the purchase and sale as a going concern of all the business assets, including furniture, fixtures and equipment, stock in trade, parts and supplies, leasehold interest and goodwill, owned by you in connection with the business carried on as _____ located at _____ .

    Subject to formal contract, we are prepared to pay $ _____ for the business on the following terms:

    If you are interested in selling at this price on these terms, please let us know and we will make you a formal offer to purchase.

                                Very truly yours,

                                _____

PURCHASE REQUIREMENT AGREEMENT

FOR GOOD CONSIDERATION, the undersigned hereby agrees to enter into this Purchase Requirement Agreement on the following terms:

1. During the period from _____ , 20___ , to _____ , 20___ , the undersigned shall purchase from Supplier goods in the following quantity: (Describe amount/time period or % of purchase requirements.)

2. The undersigned shall pay for said purchases within the Supplier's credit terms, or such extended terms as shall be expressly approved in writing by Supplier.

3. All purchases hereunder shall further be at such prices and include all promotional or advertising allowances, cash and/or trade discounts and other incentives and inducements, if any, as then customarily available to other accounts purchasing from Supplier on equally proportionate terms.

4. In the event the undersigned shall fail to meet the above described purchase requirements, or otherwise default under this agreement, then Supplier shall have full rights to demand immediate payment of all sums due Supplier notwithstanding extended terms evidenced by any note, extension agreement or other agreement authorizing extended terms.

Signed this _____ day of _____ , 20___ .

_____   _____
Customer   Supplier

PURCHASER'S ASSIGNMENT OF OPTION

In consideration of _____ Dollars ($ _____) paid to the undersigned, receipt of which is hereby acknowledged, the undersigned hereby sells, assigns, and transfers, to _____ all my right, title, and interest as purchaser in the option to purchase property dated _____, 20___, executed by _____ as seller to me as purchaser, covering certain property described as:

The undersigned represents to the Assignee that the option has not been exercised, that the period thereof will expire on _____, and that the option has not been rescinded or modified.

Signed this _____ day of _____, 20___.

In the presence of:

_____   _____
Witness   Signature of Assignor

                                   _____
                                   Name of Assignor

                                   _____
                                   Address of Assignor

                                   _____

RECEIPT

BE IT KNOWN, that the undersigned hereby acknowledges receipt of the sum of $ _____ paid by _____ which payment constitutes payment of the below described obligation:

If this is in partial payment of said obligation, the remaining unpaid balance on this date is $ _____ .

Signed this _____ day of _____ , 20___ .

Witnessed:

_____   _____
Witness   Obligor

RECEIPT FOR BALANCE OF ACCOUNT

Date:

      Received from   the sum of

Dollars ($), being the balance of account due to the undersigned as of this date.

                                                       _____

RECEIPT FOR COMPANY PROPERTY

Employee:_____

Identification No.: _____

Department/Section:_____

    I hereby acknowledge receipt of the company property listed below. I agree to keep the property in good condition and to return it when I terminate working for the company, or earlier upon request. I agree to immediately report any loss or damage to the property. In addition, I agree to use said property only for work-related purposes.

Item: _____ Received From: _____ Date: _____

Serial No.: _____ Returned To: _____ Date: _____

Item: _____ Received From: _____ Date: _____

Serial No.: _____ Returned To: _____ Date: _____

Item: _____ Received From: _____ Date: _____

Serial No.: _____ Returned To: _____ Date: _____

Item: _____ Received From: _____ Date: _____

Serial No.: _____ Returned To: _____ Date: _____

Item: _____ Received From: _____ Date: _____

Serial No.: _____ Returned To: _____ Date: _____

Item: _____ Received From: _____ Date: _____

Serial No.: _____ Returned To: _____ Date: _____

_____
Employee

_____
Date

RECEIPT IN FULL BY AN AGENT

Date:

  Received from   the sum of

Dollars ($) in full discharge of all claims which the undersigned has as of this date.

                   _____

                By:_____, Agent

RECEIPT IN FULL BY AN AGENT TO AN AGENT

Date:

Received from _____, agent for _____, the sum of _____ Dollars ($_____) in full discharge of all claims which _____ has against him or her up to date.

_____

By:_____, Agent

RECEIPT OF NOTE FOR COLLECTION

Date:

The undersigned received from   , for collection, a note dated   , 20   , signed by   and payable to   , for   Dollars ($) with interest from   , at the rate of   percent (%), which note the undersigned is to use best endeavors to collect, and to put the same in judgment at the costs of $ if not paid on presentation, to retain   percent (%) of the amount actually collected for my services, and to pay the remainder to   , but shall in no way be responsible for costs or to guarantee the collection of the same.

_____

RECEIPT ON ACCOUNT FOR GOODS TO BE DELIVERED

Date:

Received from   the sum of

Dollars ($) on account of the price of the purchase of:

to be delivered on or before   , 20   .

_____

RECEIPT ON ACCOUNT FOR PARTIAL PAYMENT

Date:

      Received from   , the sum of

Dollars ($), on account, as partial payment of the principal amount of

$.

_____

REFERENCE REPORT

Date:

To:

Re:

In reply to your request for a reference for the above-named former employee, I provide the following information:

1. Position held:_____

2. Dates employed:_____ to _____

3. Salary on termination:_____

4. Reason for termination:_____
_____
_____

5. Overall performance: _____
_____
_____

6. Other comments: _____
_____
_____

7. We would_____ would not_____ rehire.

We request that you keep this reference confidential.

                              Sincerely,

                              _____

                              Personnel Manager

RELEASE OF BREACH OF LEASE BY TENANT

Acknowledgement made this   day of   , 20   , between   (hereinafter "Landlord") and   (hereinafter "Tenant").

Whereas, by a certain lease dated   day of   , 20   , and made between Landlord and Tenant, all those premises described as

were leased to the Tenant for the term of   years from the day of   , 20   , at the yearly rent thereby reserved, and subject to the Tenant's covenant therein contained, including the following covenant:

Whereas, a breach of the said covenant has been committed, to wit, and the Landlord has agreed to execute such a release of the said breach.

Now, therefore, in consideration of $, receipt of which is acknowledged, the Landlord waives and releases all existing rights and remedies for damages, forfeiture, or otherwise which the Landlord has or could enforce against the Tenant for said breach or any other breach hereto committed and ratified and confirms said lease, provided that this waiver and release shall not extend to or prejudice any rights of the Landlord in respect of any future breaches by the Tenant.

_____
Landlord

RELEASE—INDIVIDUAL

Release executed on _____, 20___, by _____ (Releasor) to _____ (Releasee).

In consideration of _____ Dollars ($_____), receipt of which is acknowledged, Releasor voluntarily and knowingly executes this release with the express intention of effecting the extinguishment of obligations created by or arising out of:

Releasor, with the intention of binding itself, its spouse, heirs, legal representatives, and assigns, expressly releases and discharges Releasee and its heirs and legal representatives from all claims, demands, actions, judgments, and executions that Releasor ever had, or now has, or may have, known or unknown, against Releasee or its heirs or legal representatives created by or arising out of said claim.

In witness whereof, Releasor has executed this release on the day and year first above written.

_____ _____
Witness   Releasor

_____ _____
Witness   Print Name of Releasor

RENEWAL OF NOTICE OF ASSIGNMENT OF ACCOUNTS

Date:

To:

      The notice of assignment of accounts receivable, File No.   , filed on the day of   , 20   , naming   as Assignor and   as Assignee, is hereby renewed.

_____

REPLY TO APPLICANT

Date:

To:

Dear

    Thank you for your inquiry regarding employment opportunities with our company.

    Unfortunately, we do not anticipate any openings for   at the time you expect to graduate. However, we will retain the information you submitted for one year. Should an appropriate position open within that time, you will be contacted.

    Your interest in our company is appreciated. We wish you success in your job search.

                                                                    Sincerely,

                                                                    Personnel Manager

REQUEST FOR BANK CREDIT REFERENCE

Date:

To:

Re:

Dear

    The above captioned account requested we obtain a banking reference from you. So that we may evaluate proper credit for the account, we would appreciate the following information:

1. How long has the account maintained a banking relationship with you?

2. What is the account's average balance?

3. Does the account routinely overdraft?

4. Is the account a borrowing or non-borrowing account?

5. If the account borrows, please advise as to:

    Present balance on secured loans: $

    Present balance on unsecured loans: $

    Terms of repayment:

    Is repayment satisfactory?

6. Are overall banking relationships satisfactory?

    Any additional comments or information you may provide would be greatly appreciated and, of course, we would equally appreciate any future information involving a change in the account's financial situation or its banking relations with you.

    All information shall be held in the strictest confidence.

                                         Very truly yours,

_____

REQUEST FOR CREDIT INTERCHANGE

Date:

To:

Re:

Dear

The above account has recently applied to our firm for credit and listed you as a credit reference. So that we may have adequate information upon which to issue credit, we request the benefit of your credit experience with the account by providing us the following information:

High Credit: $

Low Credit: $

Terms:

How long sold:

Present balance owed: $

Payment history:

Any other credit information you believe helpful may be noted on the reverse side and shall be held strictly confidential. We are always pleased to reciprocate.

A stamped return envelope is enclosed for your convenience.

Very truly yours,

_____

REQUEST FOR INFORMATION ON OVERDUE ACCOUNT

Date:

To:

Re:
    (Account)

We have not received payment on your overdue account and would appreciate it if you take a moment to explain why. Please check the applicable reason and return to this office:

_____ We need copies of unpaid invoices: _____

_____ We have credits outstanding: _____

_____ Payment has been mailed on _____, 20___ .

_____ Payment will be mailed on _____, 20___ .

_____ Other: _____

Please use the reverse side if more space is needed.

Thank you for your immediate attention.

Very truly,

_____

REQUEST FOR PREPAYMENT

Date:

To:

Thank you for your order dated   , 20   . We regret to inform you that we cannot ship the products ordered on credit or on C.O.D. terms for the following reason:

However, we would be pleased to promptly process and ship your order upon prepayment of the order in the amount of $.

We look forward to your payment so that we may expedite your order.

Again, we thank you for your cooperation and patronage.

                    Very truly,

                    _____

REQUEST FOR REFERENCE

Date:

To:

Re:

The above-named individual has applied for a position with our company and indicates previous employment with your firm. The information requested below will help us to evaluate the applicant. We will hold your comments in strict confidence. Thank you for your cooperation.

                    Sincerely,

                    Personnel Department

Please Indicate:

Position With Your Firm: _____

Employed From _____ Through _____

Final Salary $_____ Social Insurance No. _____

Please rate the applicant on the basis of his/her employment with you (good/fair/poor):

Ability_____ Conduct_____ Attitude _____

Efficiency _____ Attendance_____ Punctuality _____

What was the reason for termination? _____

_____

Would you re-hire? _____ If not, give reason: _____

_____

                                            _____
                                            Signature and Title

REQUEST FOR TRANSCRIPT

Date:

To:

    Please be advised that I am being considered for employment by _____ and in order to complete my application they have requested a copy of my school transcript.

    Please send a transcript to the following:

        Firm: _____

        Address: _____

        _____

        Attention: _____

Thank you.

                                        Sincerely,

                                        _____

                                        _____

Attended: _____ to _____
                      (month & year)   (month & year)

Degree/Diploma Received: _____

Enclosed is $ _____ to cover cost of transcript.

REQUEST TO INSPECT PERSONNEL FILE

Employee: _____ Date Requested: _____

Social Insurance Number: _____

Department/Location: _____

Work Phone: _____

I request an appointment with the Personnel Department for the purpose of inspecting my personnel file.

I previously reviewed my file: _____

_____   _____
Signature   Date

File review appointment scheduled for:

Date: _____   Time: _____

Location: _____

Date File Review Completed: _____

Employee comments regarding information in the personnel file:

_____
_____
_____
_____

_____   _____
Personnel Representative   Date

_____   _____
Employee Signature   Date

Employee should complete top section of request form and forward to the Personnel Department. Place one completed copy of this form into personnel file upon completion of review.

REQUEST TO REDUCE BALANCE

Date:

To:

We often assist customers who exceed their credit limit by suggesting payment plans which can help reduce their outstanding balance.

Your account balance is $ as of the last statement date. The balance has remained at this level for quite some time.

We would like to see your balance reduced to $, and suggest you accomplish it by remaining current on future purchases, and pay $ each month toward the present balance. This will reduce your balance to the approved credit limit without seriously affecting your cash flow.

We hope this payment plan is suitable for you, and will call you to confirm this arrangement.

Very truly,

_____

RESIDENTIAL RENTAL APPLICATION

Name of Applicant _____ Telephone _____

Present Address _____

City, Province, Postal Code _____

Social Ins. No. _____ Spouse's Soc. Ins. No. _____

Credit Cards (issuer & acct.#) _____ _____

How many in your family?   Adults _____   Children _____   Any Pets? _____

Number of Occupants _____

How long have you lived at the present address? _____

Present Landlord _____ Telephone _____

Prior Landlord _____ Telephone _____

Employer _____ Your Position _____

How long? _____ Contact _____ Telephone _____

Salary _____ Amt. & source additional income _____

Name of Bank

_____ Chequeing Account No. _____

_____ Savings Account No. _____

Additional Personal/Credit References

Name	Relationship	Telephone
_____	_____	_____
_____	_____	_____
_____	_____	_____

    I represent that the information provided in this application is true to the best of my knowledge. You are hereby authorized to verify my credit and employment references in connection with the processing of this application. I acknowledge receipt of a copy of this application.

Dated: _____

_____
Applicant

RESIGNATION

Date:

To:

Please be informed that I hereby submit my resignation in all capacities with the company effective:

Pursuant to company policy and/or the terms of my employment, I shall make appropriate arrangements for the return of company property.

Any compensation due me or other correspondence may be directed to me at:

Sincerely,

_____

RESUME ACKNOWLEDGEMENT

Date:

To:

Thank you for your correspondence and resume concerning a position with our firm.

We do want to inform you that your information is being reviewed for employment consideration. We will contact you for an interview if your qualifications meet our current needs.

We appreciate your interest in our firm.

Sincerely,

_____
Personnel Manager

RETIREMENT CHECKLIST

Employee: _____ Department: _____

1. Letter of Resignation—Submit a Letter of Resignation indicating the starting date of your upcoming retirement to your supervisor who will forward it to the Human Resources Department. Please include your forwarding address in your letter.

2. Vacation Pay—All vacation earned but not taken prior to retirement will be included in your final pay.

3. Address Change—Your address will be changed automatically when you retire and you will receive your statements at home.

4. Employee Benefits—Contact the Employee Benefits Department for information concerning your continued benefit coverage, as well as accrued benefits.

5. Company Property—If you have been issued any of the following, please arrange to return them to your supervisor:

    _____ Security badge   _____ Supervisor's manual

    _____ ID badge   _____ Keys

    _____ Other _____

RETURN OF CLAIM AS NONCOLLECTIBLE

Date:

To:

Despite our repeated efforts, we have been unable to collect your claim against _____. Since you have not authorized us to turn your accounts over to our lawyers for litigation, we are returning this claim to you as noncollectible.

_____

REVOCATION OF GUARANTY

Date:

To:

    Reference is made to our guaranty dated _____, 20___, issued to you by the undersigned guaranteeing the continued credit of _____ (Obligor).

    Please be advised that effective upon receipt of this letter of guaranty (or such effective date as provided under the guaranty), the undersigned shall not be obligated under the guaranty for any future or further credit extended by you to the Obligor. We understand that we shall remain liable for the present balance until paid.

    We would appreciate confirmation of the present balance owed and would further appreciate notification when said balance has been fully paid.

    Please confirm to us in writing receipt and acknowledgement of this guaranty revocation by return acknowledgement below.

    Thank you for your cooperation.

                                   Very truly yours,

                                   _____

Acknowledged:

_____

Effective Date:_____

SALE ON APPROVAL ACKNOWLEDGEMENT

Date:

To:

We acknowledge the goods delivered on the attached invoice or order were sold on a sale-on-approval basis.

In the event you are not satisfied with the goods you have the right to return all or any part thereof at our expense within _____ days of receipt for full credit (or refund if prepaid).

Goods not returned within that time shall be deemed accepted, and there shall be no further right of return.

We thank you for your business and hope the goods will prove satisfactory and meet with your approval.

                                                Very truly yours,

_____

SALES REPRESENTATIVE AGREEMENT

Agreement between

(Company) and

(Sales Representative).

SALES REPRESENTATIVE AGREES TO:

1. Represent and sell the Company's _____ products/services in the geographic area of _____.
2. Accurately represent and state Company policies to all potential and present customers.
3. Promptly mail all leads and orders to the Company.
4. Inform the sales manager of all problems concerning Company customers within the sales territory.
5. Inform the sales manager if the Sales Representative is representing, or plans to represent, any other business firm. In no event shall Sales Representative represent a competitive company or product line either within or outside the designated sales area.
6. Telephone the Company with reasonable frequency to discuss sales activity within the territory.
7. Provide Company 30-days' notice should the Representative intend to terminate this agreement.
8. Return promptly all materials and samples provided by the Company to the Representative, if either party terminates this agreement.

THE COMPANY AGREES TO:

1. Pay the following commissions to the Sales Representative:
    (a) ____ percent of all prepaid sales, except as stated in (4) below
    (b) ____ percent of all credit sales, except as stated in (4) below

2. To negotiate in advance of sale the commission percentage to be paid on all orders that the Company allows a quantity discount or other trade concession.

3. Commissions on refunds to customers or merchandise returned by the customer in which a commission has already been paid to the Representative shall be deducted from future commissions to be paid to the Representative by the Company.

4. Except by special arrangement, the following shall not be commissioned:

5. To provide the Sales Representative with reasonable quantities of business cards, brochures, catalogs, and any product samples required for sales purposes.

6. To set minimum monthly quotas after consultation with the Sales Representative.

7. To grant Representative 30-days' notice should the Company wish to terminate this agreement.

8. To pay commissions to the Representative on sales from existing customers for a period of ( ) months after this agreement is terminated by either party.

9. This constitutes the entire agreement.

10. This agreement shall be binding upon the parties and their successors and assigns.

Signed this   day of   , 20   .

_____   _____
Company   Sales Representative

SAMPLE LETTER
REQUESTING AN OUT OF COURT SETTLEMENT

Attn: Credit Manager

Dear

    Due to recent unemployment and illness in the family, I have found it impossible to pay my debts in full. My present income leaves nothing for back bills, and I have no assets or personal possessions to either sell or borrow against.

    Considering the extent of my total indebtedness, it will be impossible to pay them fully, and therefore I am offering to pay creditors _____ % on the dollar (in _____ installments of _____ % each) in full settlement and satisfaction of the debt owed. This proposal is being made this date to all my creditors.

    If this is acceptable to you, please sign one copy of this letter, and return for my records.

    I regret this action is necessary. However I am confident it will enable my creditors to receive more than could be obtained under bankruptcy and, therefore, you will join with other creditors in accepting this plan.

    Thank you for your cooperation.

Sincerely,

Accepted:

_____
Creditor

Date:

SAMPLE LETTER REQUESTING INSTALLMENT PAYMENTS

Attn: Credit Manager

Dear

  Due to recent unemployment and illness in the family, I have found it impossible to pay my debts as they fall due and therefore find it necessary to propose payment of my indebtedness to you in the amount of $ _____ in _____ monthly installments of $ _____ each.

  I have attached my monthly budget which discloses I have only $ _____ available each month (after necessary living expenses) and this must be applied to my total indebtedness of approximately $ _____ . Therefore, under my proposed plan, each of my creditors shall receive an equally proportionate payment each month.

  As you can understand, I have made significant sacrifice in my living standard to arrange this payment plan. I am equally confident you share my view that your patience in receiving payment is far preferable to a forced bankruptcy that would yield little or nothing for creditors.

  If this proposed installment plan is satisfactory, please sign and return one copy of this letter for my record. Payments will commence on the first day of the following month.

  I appreciate your understanding and cooperation.

Sincerely,

Accepted:

_____
Creditor
Date:

SAMPLES AND DOCUMENTS RECEIPT

I, _____, employed in the position of _____, confirm that I have received from my employer the following samples:

No. Rec'd.	Serial No.	Description	Value Each	Total Value
_____	_____	_____	_____	_____
_____	_____	_____	_____	_____
_____	_____	_____	_____	_____
_____	_____	_____	_____	_____
_____	_____	_____	_____	_____
_____	_____	_____	_____	_____

I further confirm that I have received the following documents:

I accept responsibility to safeguard these materials, prevent the disclosure of confidential material, and return these (except those authorized for and delivered to customers) to my employer upon demand and, in any event, upon termination of employment.

_____
Employee

_____
Date

SCHEDULE OF ASSETS FOR SALE OR LOAN

Asset	Fair Market Value	Loan Value
_____	$ _____	$ _____
_____	$ _____	$ _____
_____	$ _____	$ _____
_____	$ _____	$ _____
_____	$ _____	$ _____
_____	$ _____	$ _____
_____	$ _____	$ _____
_____	$ _____	$ _____
_____	$ _____	$ _____
_____	$ _____	$ _____
_____	$ _____	$ _____
_____	$ _____	$ _____
_____	$ _____	$ _____
_____	$ _____	$ _____
_____	$ _____	$ _____
_____	$ _____	$ _____
_____	$ _____	$ _____
_____	$ _____	$ _____
_____	$ _____	$ _____
_____	$ _____	$ _____
_____	$ _____	$ _____
_____	$ _____	$ _____

SECOND NOTICE OF OVERDUE ACCOUNT

Date:

To:

Dear

There can be no better way to show you why we are concerned about your overdue account than to list your account balance.

PAST DUE

Over 30 Days	$_____
Over 60 days	$_____
Over 90 days	$_____
Total	$_____

May we now have your cheque without further delay.

Very truly yours,

_____

SECOND WARNING NOTICE

Employee: _____ Employee No.: _____

Shift: _____ Date of warning: _____

Date of violation: _____ Time of violation: _____

Violation

____ Intoxication or drugs ____ Substandard work ____ Disobedience

____ Clocking out ahead of time ____ Wrongful conduct ____ Tardiness

____ Clocking out wrong time card ____ Carelessness ____ Absenteeism

____ Other: _____

Action Taken: _____
_____
_____

Additional Remarks: _____
_____
_____

Employee Comments: _____
_____
_____

This is your second warning of a company rules violation or unsatisfactory performance. Future violations may lead to immediate dismissal without further notice.

_____
Employee

_____
Supervisor

_____
Personnel Manager

SETTLEMENT OF DISPUTED ACCOUNT

Whereas,   (Creditor) asserts to hold a certain claim against   (Debtor) in the amount of $ arising from: (Describe obligation)

Whereas, Debtor disputes said claim, and

Whereas, the parties desire to resolve and forever settle said claim.

Now, therefore, Debtor agrees to pay to Creditor and Creditor agrees to accept from Debtor simultaneous herewith, the sum of
Dollars ($) in full payment, settlement, satisfaction and discharge of said claim and in release of any further claims thereto.

This agreement shall be binding upon and inure to the benefit of the parties, their successors, assigns and personal representatives.

Signed this   day of   , 20   .

Witnessed:

_____   _____
                                                          Creditor

_____   _____
                                                            Debtor

SETTLEMENT OFFER ON DISPUTED ACCOUNT

Date:

To:

Re:

We dispute your reasons for nonpayment on your account in the amount of $.

However, we are prepared to accept an immediate payment of $ in full settlement of your disputed account. Please understand that this settlement offer is solely for the purpose of a quick resolution of this undesired matter, and in no way is an admission of liability.

If this proposal is acceptable to you, please promptly send the requested payment by return mail.

Sincerely,

_____

SIGHT DRAFT

Date:

To:

Dear

      Upon presentment, you are directed to debit our account and pay to the order of the sum of

Dollars ($).

_____
Account Name

By:_____
     Authorized Signature

_____
Account Number

SPECIFIC GUARANTY

FOR GOOD AND VALUABLE CONSIDERATION, and as an inducement for _____ of _____ (Creditor), to extend credit to _____ of _____ (Borrower), the undersigned jointly, severally and unconditionally guarantee to Creditor the prompt and full payment of the following obligation:

And the undersigned agree to remain bound on this guaranty notwithstanding any extension, renewal, indulgence, forbearance or waiver, or release, discharge or substitution of any collateral or security for the obligation. In the event of default, the Creditor may seek payment directly from the undersigned without need to proceed first against Borrower, and the undersigned waive all suretyship defenses.

The obligations of the undersigned under this guarantee shall be only to the specific debt described and to no other debt or obligation between Borrower and Creditor.

In the event of default, the guarantor shall be responsible for all lawyers' fees and reasonable costs of collection.

This guaranty shall be binding upon and inure to the benefit of the parties, their successors, assigns and personal representatives.

Signed this _____ day of _____, 20____.

In the Presence of:

_____   _____
Witness   Creditor

_____   _____
Witness   Borrower

                                                              _____
                                                              Borrower

SPECIFIC RELEASE

BE IT KNOWN, for good consideration, the undersigned, Releasor(s),

of   ,

jointly and severally hereby forever release, discharge and acquit

of   ,

from any and all contracts, claims, suits, actions or liabilities both in law and in equity specifically arising from, relating to or otherwise described as and limited to:

This release applies only to the foregoing matters and extends to no other debt, account, agreement, obligations, cause of action, liability or undertaking by and between the parties, which, if existing, shall survive this release and remain in full force and effect and undisturbed by this specific release.

This release shall be binding upon and inure to the benefit of the parties, their successors, assigns and personal representatives.

Signed this   day of   , 20   .

Witnessed:

_____   _____
Witness   Releasor

_____   _____
Witness   Print Name of Releasor

STATEMENT OF WISHES

OF

_____

I, _____ , do hereby set forth certain wishes and requests to my Executor/Executrix/Trustee, heirs, family, friends and others who may carry out these wishes. I understand these wishes are advisory only and not mandatory.

My wishes are:

Dated:

_____
Signature

STOCK SUBSCRIPTION

I, _____ , the undersigned do hereby subscribe for the purchase of (   ) shares of the common stock of _____ (Corporation), for the aggregate purchase price of $. I understand that upon issue, said shares shall constitute   % of the common shares outstanding and entitled to vote and that there are no other shares outstanding.

_____

The foregoing subscription is accepted and the Treasurer shall issue said shares upon payment to the corporation the sum of $.

_____
For the Corporation
and its Board of Directors

SUBLEASE

Sublease agreement entered into between

of _____ (Tenant),

of _____ (Subtenant) and

_____ of _____ (Landlord).

SUBLEASE PERIOD: The Subtenant agrees to sublease from Tenant property known as _____ from _____, 20___, to _____, 20___.

TERMS OF SUBLEASE: The Subtenant agrees to comply with all terms and conditions of the lease entered into by the Tenant, including the prompt payment of all rents. The lease terms are incorporated into this agreement by reference. The Subtenant agrees to pay the Landlord the monthly rent stated in that lease, and all other rental charges hereinafter due, and otherwise assume all of Tenant's obligations during the Sublease period and to indemnify Tenant from any liability arising from Subtenant's breach.

SECURITY DEPOSIT: The Subtenant agrees to pay to Tenant the sum of $_____ as a security deposit, to be promptly returned upon the termination of this sublease and compliance of all conditions of this sublease.

INVENTORY: Attached to this agreement is an inventory of items or fixtures on the above described property on _____, 20___. The Subtenant agrees to replace or reimburse the Tenant for any of these items that are missing or damaged.

LANDLORD'S CONSENT: The Landlord consents to this sublease and agrees to promptly notify the Tenant at

if the Subtenant is in breach of this agreement. Nothing herein shall constitute a release of Tenant who shall remain bound under this lease. Nothing herein shall constitute a consent to any further Sublease or Assignment of Lease.

Date:

_____
Landlord

_____
Subtenant

_____
Tenant

SUMMARY OF EMPLOYMENT TERMS

Date:

To:

We are very pleased you have accepted a position with our company. The following is a summary of your initial terms and conditions of employment.

1. Commencement date of employment: _____

2. Position/title: _____

3. Starting salary: _____

4. Weeks vacation/year: _____

5. Eligible for vacation starting: _____

6. Health insurance: _____
   _____

7. Pension/profit-sharing: _____
   _____

8. Other benefits: _____
   _____

9. Other terms/conditions: _____
   _____

If this does not accurately summarize your understanding, please notify me immediately. You understand, of course, that your employment may be terminated by either party at will, and we reserve the right to modify benefits, terms of employment, and employee policies.

Again, we look forward to your joining us.

Sincerely,

_____

SUSPENSION WITHOUT PAY NOTICE

Date:

To:

Dear

    This letter is to inform you that you are hereby suspended from your job for _____ working days commencing _____, 20___. This disciplinary action is being taken based on the following facts:

    Your conduct as described above constitutes sufficient cause for disciplinary action. In addition, you have been disciplined previously for the same problem.

    Your formal disciplinary action is:

    A copy of this letter will be placed in your personnel file. You have the right to respond in writing to present information or arguments rebutting this suspension. If you choose to respond, you have until _____ .m. on _____, 20___ to do so. Your response, if any, will be considered prior to the imposition of the proposed suspension. It will be assumed that you have waived the right to respond if you do not take advantage of the above alternative.

    The purpose of this suspension is to impress upon you the seriousness with which we regard the above violation of employment conditions and to give you the opportunity to reflect upon your future compliance with our employment standards. If you continue to violate the conditions of your employment, you may be terminated.

Sincerely,

_____

TEMPORARY EMPLOYMENT REQUISITION

To:

Date:

Number of Temporary Employees Needed: _____

Position(s)/Duties: _____

Department: _____

Supervisor: _____

Starting Dates: _____ to _____

Shift _____ to _____

Reasons for Requisition: _____

_____

_____

_____

_____

_____

Estimated Cost: _____

Budget Number: _____

Budgeted?   yes _____ no _____

_____   _____
Signed By   Date

_____   _____
Approved By   Date

Temporary personnel are not allowed employment beyond approval period or for an amount above estimated expense, unless approved in advance.

TENANT'S NOTICE TO EXERCISE PURCHASE OPTION

Date:

To:

Dear

    Notice is hereby provided that the undersigned as Lessee under a certain Lease dated _____, 20____, does hereby exercise its purchase option under said lease to purchase the property described as

for the option price of $_____.

    As contained within the lease agreement, I enclose $_____ as a deposit toward said purchase option.

_____
Lessee (Tenant)

REGISTERED MAIL

TENANT'S NOTICE TO TERMINATE TENANCY

Date:

To:

Please be advised that as your tenant on certain premises described as:

I/we hereby notify you of my/our intention to terminate my/our tenancy effective _____, 20___. On or before said date, I/we shall deliver to you full possession of the premises, together with the keys, and if applicable I/we request prompt return of any security deposit or escrow that you may be holding.

Thank you for your cooperation.

_____
Tenant

_____
Tenant

_____
Address

REGISTERED MAIL

TERMINATION CHECKLIST

Employee: _____ Date: _____

Department: _____

    _____ Voluntary

    _____ Involuntary

    _____ With Notice

    _____ Without Notice

Reason: _____

_____

_____ Eligible for rehire?

_____ Vacation pay period?

_____ Transfer to referral status? (will need Referral Agreement)

_____ Resignation/Separation Notice completed

_____ License information

_____ Return of all company property, including keys and parking pass, telephone codes, credit cards, personnel manual

_____ Paycheque delivered to employee upon termination

_____
Supervisor

_____
Date

TERMINATION LETTER FOR EXCESSIVE ABSENTEEISM

Date:

To:

Dear

As stated in my letter to you of   , your record of absence from work has kept you from performing the full schedule of assignments for your position. I further indicated that a continuation of absences could lead to your termination.

A current review of your attendance indicates that since that warning you have been absent from work for   out of the last   days.

In view of your poor attendance record, I am recommending to the Personnel Director, by copy of this letter, that your employment with the company be terminated effective   , 20   .

Should you desire to meet for the purpose of discussing this intended action, please notify us within ten working days after receipt of this letter.

Sincerely,

_____

TERMINATION LETTER FOR INTOXICATION ON THE JOB

Date:

To:

Dear

    This letter is to inform you that we are terminating your employment effective _____. This decision is based on an incident report submitted to me on _____ by your supervisor, _____. The report recommended your termination because of your intoxication during working hours.

    As you are aware, the first reported incident of your intoxication on the job was _____. That report was placed in your personnel file, and you were informed at that time that another incident would result in a disciplinary action or possible dismissal.

    This second incident of intoxication adversely affected the operational efficiency and effectiveness of your department and threatened the safety of other employees.

    Your final paycheque, including all forms of compensation due you, may be picked up in the Personnel Office on your way out.

                                                     Sincerely,

                                                     Personnel Manager

TIME NOTE

FOR VALUE RECEIVED, the undersigned promise to pay to the order of _____, the sum of _____ Dollars ($_____), payable with annual interest of _____% on any unpaid balance.

All principal and accrued interest shall be fully due and payable on _____, 20___, time being of the essence.

This note may be prepaid, in whole or in part, without penalty.

All parties to this note waive presentment, demand, protest or notices thereto and agree to remain bound notwithstanding any indulgence, modification or release or discharge of any party or collateral securing this note. The undersigned shall be jointly and severally liable under this note.

Upon default, the undersigned agree to pay all reasonable lawyers' fees and costs of collection.

Signed this _____ day of _____, 20___.

Signed in the presence of:

_____   _____
Witness   Maker

_____   _____
Witness   Maker

TRANSMITTAL FOR COLLECTION

Date:

To:
    (Lawyer)

    We enclose our file on the following unpaid accounts and request collection of same. We shall pay your standard fees and costs.

    Account Name(s)   Balance Owed

    Please provide us with interim reports on your collection progress.

               Very truly yours,

               _____

TRIP PERMISSION

The undersigned _____, referred to as Parent, is the parent and lawful guardian of _____, a minor.

Parent acknowledges that said minor is authorized to take the following trip _____, sponsored by _____, and to engage in all activities incident thereto.

Parent hereby appoints _____ as *loco parentis*, and is authorized to render such emergency medical care to _____ as could be undertaken by the parent, and the parent hereby releases said _____, and its agents and employees from any and all acts taken in good faith during the trip.

Signed this _____ day of _____, 20____.

In the presence of:

_____   _____
Witness   Parent

UNSOLICITED IDEA ACKNOWLEDGEMENT

To:

Dear

      We appreciate your interest in submitting for our consideration an idea or proposal relative to:

      Our company receives many commercial ideas, suggestions and proposals, and also has many of its own projects under development or consideration. Therefore, it is possible the idea or proposal you plan to submit to us has been considered and/or may already be in the planning or development stages.

      Therefore, we would be pleased to accept your idea or proposal for consideration provided you acknowledge:

1. Samples or other submissions will be returned only if return postage or freight is prepaid.

2. The company accepts no responsibility for casualty or loss to samples or other submitted material in our possession.

3. The company accepts no responsibility for holding any submitted information in confidence, but shall use its best efforts to hold it confidential.

4. The company shall pay compensation only in the event it a) accepts the submitted idea, b) has received the idea only from you, and c) reaches agreement with you as to terms and conditions.

5. Company agrees not to exploit said idea, directly or indirectly, without first entering into a compensation agreement acceptable to you.

6. Nothing in this agreement shall be deemed to give company any rights in the materials submitted.

7. Company shall have no obligation to you in the event this idea or material is presently under consideration by company.

If these terms are acceptable to you, please sign where indicated below and submit with your idea or proposal.

_____

The foregoing terms and conditions are understood and acknowledged this day of   , 20   .

In the presence of:

_____   _____
Witness   Submitter

VERIFICATION OF EDUCATION

Date:

To:

Re:

The above individual has applied to our organization for employment.

According to the information in the employment application, this individual has attended your school. Would you please verify the above by completing the following information:

Dates Attended:_____

Still Attending? _____

Degree/Diploma Earned: _____

Grade Point Average:_____

Honors or Commendations: _____

Other Comments:_____

_____

Your cooperation in completing and returning this in the self-enclosed envelope is greatly appreciated.

Very truly yours,

_____

VERIFICATION OF EMPLOYMENT

Date:

Re:

Dear

The individual identified above is being evaluated for employment and has signed our employment application authorizing this inquiry. We would appreciate a statement of your experiences with this person when employed by your company. Please provide the information requested on the bottom of this letter and return to us in the enclosed self-addressed, stamped envelope at your earliest convenience. Your reply will be held in strict confidence. We sincerely appreciate your cooperation and will gladly reciprocate.

                    Sincerely,

_____

CONFIDENTIAL

Applicant Name: _____

Address: _____

Name of Former Company: _____

Address: _____

Employed From: _____ To: _____

General Work Record: _____

_____

_____

_____

_____
                    Signature

VERIFICATION OF LICENSURE

Date:

To:

Please be advised that as a condition of my employment with   ,
I hereby authorize release of information relative to the status of my license or registration as a
within the Province of   .

Please certify below and return to:

    Firm   _____

    Address   _____
                        _____

    Attn: _____

Thank you.

_____

CERTIFICATION

This will certify that the above,   , is duly licensed in the Province of
                         as a   , and said license or
registration is in good standing with no disciplinary or revocation proceedings pending.

Dated:

_____
Certifying Official

WAIVER AND ASSUMPTION OF RISK

The undersigned, _____ (Customer), voluntarily makes and grants this Waiver and Assumption of Risk in favor of _____ (Seller) as partial consideration in addition to monies paid to Seller for the opportunity to use the facilities, equipment, materials and/or other assets of Seller, and/or to receive assistance, training, guidance, tutelage and/or instruction from the personnel of Seller, and/or to engage in the activities, events, sports, festivities and/or gatherings sponsored by Seller. I do hereby waive and release any and all claims whether in contract or of personal injury, bodily injury, property damage, damages, losses and/or death that may arise from my aforementioned use or receipt, as I understand and recognize that there are certain risks, dangers and perils connected with such use and/or receipt which I hereby acknowledge have been fully explained to me and which I fully understand, and which I nevertheless accept, assume and undertake after inquiry and investigation of extent, duration, and completeness wholly satisfactory and acceptable to me. I further agree to use my best judgment in undertaking these activities, use and/or receipt and to faithfully adhere to all safety instructions and recommendations, whether oral or written. I hereby certify that I am a competent adult assuming these risks of my own free will, being under no compulsion or duress. This Waiver and Assumption of Risk is effective from _____, 20___, to _____, 20___, inclusive, and may not be revoked, altered, amended, rescinded or voided without the express prior written consent of Seller.

_____   _____
Print Name   Date

_____   _____
Customer's Signature   Age

_____   _____
Address

WAIVER OF LIABILITY

I, _____ (Employee), hereby release _____ (Company) from any and all liability connected with my participation in company recreational activities. I acknowledge that I am participating in these activities on my own time and of my own choice and assume all risk in connection thereto.

_____
Employee

_____
Date

_____
Witness

WAIVER OF NOTICE OF ANNUAL MEETING
BY INDIVIDUAL SHAREHOLDER

      I, the undersigned, the holder of   shares of stock of   ,
do hereby waive notice of the annual meeting of shareholders of the
Corporation which will be held for the following purposes:

    (1)   Electing a new board of directors.

    (2)   Transacting any other business that may properly be brought before the meeting.

    The undersigned hereby consents to the holding of the meeting on   ,
20   , at   .m. at the offices of the Corporation which are located at
    , in the City of   .

Date: _____

WAIVER OF NOTICE OF DIRECTORS' MEETING

The undersigned, constituting the entire membership of the Board of Directors of _____, hereby waive notice of the meeting of the Board of Directors of the Corporation and consent to the holding of the meeting at _____ .m. on _____, 20___, at the offices of the Corporation located at _____. Furthermore, we agree that any lawful business may be transacted at the meeting.

Dated:

_____

_____

_____

WAIVER OF NOTICE OF ORGANIZATION MEETING OF INCORPORATORS AND DIRECTORS OF

_____

We do hereby constitute the Incorporators and Directors of the above captioned Corporation and do hereby waive notice of the organization meeting of Directors and Incorporators of the said Corporation.

Furthermore, we hereby agree that said meeting shall be held at   o'clock   .m. on   , 20   , at the following location:

                                                                                                                        .

We do hereby affix our names to show our waiver of notice of said meeting.

Dated:

_____   _____

_____   _____

WAIVER OF NOTICE—COMBINED MEETING

      I, the undersigned, the holder of _____ shares of stock of _____ and/or a Board Director, do hereby waive notice of the combined meeting of shareholders and board of directors of the said corporation.

      Furthermore, the undersigned hereby agrees that said meeting shall be held at _____ .m. on _____, 20____, at the following location:

Date: _____   _____

WARRANTY BILL OF SALE

BE IT KNOWN, that for good consideration, and in payment of the sum of $, the receipt and sufficiency of which is acknowledged, the undersigned
of   (Seller) hereby sells and transfers to
                                          of
(Buyer) and its successors and assigns forever, the following described chattels and personal property:

Seller warrants to Buyer it has good and marketable title to said property, full authority to sell and transfer said property, and that said property is sold free of all liens, encumbrances, liabilities and adverse claims of every nature and description whatsoever.

Seller further warrants to Buyer that it will fully defend, protect, indemnify and hold harmless the Buyer and its lawful successors and assigns from any adverse claim thereto.

Said assets are otherwise sold in "as is" condition and where presently located.

Signed this   day of   , 20   .

In the presence of:

_____   _____
Signature of Witness   Signature of Seller

_____   _____
Print Name of Witness   Print Name of Seller

_____   _____
Address of Witness   Address of Seller

_____   _____

WITHHELD DELIVERY NOTICE

Date:

To:

Dear

Reference is made to your order for certain goods under date of   ,
20   , as per your Purchase Order No.

We are withholding delivery for the reason(s) checked:

_____ Overdue balance of $_____ must first be paid.

_____ Required payment of $_____ has not been made.

_____ You previously withdrew your order.

_____ You failed to furnish required shipping instructions.

_____ Certain goods are back ordered and shipment will be made in single lot.

_____ Other: _____

Please respond to this notice so we may fulfill your order without further delay or inconvenience.

Very truly yours,

_____

WRITTEN UNANIMOUS CONSENT IN LIEU OF MEETING

The undersigned, being the holders of all of the outstanding shares of _____ Corporation entitled to vote at a meeting of shareholders, do hereby consent to the following resolution adopted by the Board of Directors of _____ Corporation taken on _____, 20___:

Dated:

Signed:_____

_____

_____

GLOSSARY

—A—

Absence Request—
Documents approved or denied absence.

Acceptance of Claim—
Collection agency agreement.

Accident Claim Notice—
Notice to insurance agency of claim due to an accident.

Acknowledged Receipt of Goods—
Unconditional acceptance of goods.

Acknowledgement of Modified Terms—
Response to changes in a contract.

Acknowledgement of Temporary Employment—
Agreement to terms of temporary employee status.

Addendum to Contract—
Adds or modifies terms to a contract.

Addendum to Employment Agreement—
Use to change an employment agreement.

Address Change Notice—
Notifies all parties of a change of address.

Agreement of Waiver of Right of Inheritance—
A beneficiary under a will gives up his or her right to inherit.

Agreement on Proprietary Rights—
Outlines a company policy on proprietary rights.

Agreement Reminder—
Reminds a debtor of a promise to pay.

Agreement to Accept Night Work—
Outlines company policy on night work.

Agreement to Assume Debt—
Agrees to transfer debt to third party.

Agreement to Compromise Debt—
Agrees to reduce customer's indebtedness.

Agreement to Extend Debt Payment—
Agrees to increase time to pay debt.

Agreement to Extend Performance Date—
Written notice to contractor extending time to complete project.

Agreement to Extend Period of Option—
Written notice to option holder extending time to exercise option.

Agreement to Lease—
Usually used for commercial property.

Agreement to Purchase Stock—
Written contract outlining terms of buying stock.

Agreement to Sell Personal Property—
Usually used for the sale of any kind of property other than real estate.

Amendment to Lease—
Written changes to lease terms.

Analysis of Cash Available for Debt Repayment—
Use to plan a budget.

Applicant Acknowledgement—
Use to arrange interview with a job applicant.

Applicant Interview Confirmation—
Confirms appointment for interview.

Applicant Notification—
Notifies applicant of unsuccessful attempts to be contacted.

Applicant Referral Program—
Use to refer one employee by another.

Applicant Waiver—
Applicant agrees to be bound by the rules and regulations of the company.

Assignment by Endorsing on Lease—
Use to sublease commercial property.

Assignment of Accounts Receivable with Non-Recourse—
Turns over uncollected income to a third party with no guarantee of payment.

Assignment of Accounts Receivable with Recourse—
Relinquishes uncollected income to a third party who guarantees payment.

Assignment of Assets—
Gives control of assets to a third party.

Assignment of Bank Account—
Gives the contents of a bank account to a third party.

Assignment of Contract—
Turns over contract obligation to a third party who must fulfill those obligations.

Assignment of Damage Claim—
Gives right to claim damages to a third party.

Assignment of Income—
Transfers income from debtor to creditor.

Assignment of Insurance Policy—
Gives benefits of policy to third party.

Assignment of Lease—
Turns over lease to a third party.

Assignment of Money Due—
Gives a third party the right to collect money owed.

Assignment of Option—
Transfers the right to exercise option to third party.

Authorization to Release Confidential Information—
Gives company or individual approval to issue confidential information.

Authorization to Release Credit Information—
Gives company approval to issue information about your credit to others.

Authorization to Release Employment Information—
Approves the release of job information.

Authorization to Release Financial Statements—
Authorizes release of company's financial statements to a third party.

Authorization to Release Information—
Gives general approval to release information.

Authorization to Release Medical Information—
Used to notify doctors, hospitals, and insurance companies of approval to release medical information.

Authorization to Return Goods—
Seller approves return of goods shipped to buyer.

Bad Cheque Notice—
Company holding bad cheque notifies cheque writer to pay in cash.

Balloon Note—
Agreement to borrow money and repay in lump sum.

Bill of Sale—
Document showing all parties to a sale, the type of property sold, and the price.

Breach of Contract Notice—
Notice sent to party of contract specifying the terms violated.

Cancellation of Stop-Payment Order—
Notice to bank to cancel stop payment order.

Certificate of Corporate Resolution—
Authorizes specific corporate action.

Change of Beneficiary—
Notifies insurance company of a new person to benefit from your policy.

Change Work Order—
Written revisions to a contract to perform specific tasks, such as construction of a building.

Cheque Stop-Payment—
Request to bank to not honor a particular cheque.

Child Guardianship Consent Form—
Appoints a guardian and specifies their powers.

Cohabitation Agreement—
Outlines rights of two parties seeking to live together.

Commercial Lease—
Agreement to rent commercial property.

Confidentiality Agreement—
Agreement between two or more parties to keep certain information secret.

Confirmation of Verbal Agreement—
Use for a verbal agreement with new payment terms.

Confirmation of Verbal Order—
Letter from buyer confirming placement of order with seller.

Conflict of Interest Declaration—
Employee declares no conflict of interest with present employer.

Consent for Drug/Alcohol Screen Testing—
Agreement by employee authorizing company to take tests.

Consent to Assignment—
Owner of property or contract agrees to transfer of rights to a third party.

Consent to Partial Assignment—
Owner of contract or property agrees to partial transfer of rights or obligations.

Consent to Release of Information—
Employee agrees to the release of specific confidential information.

Consignment Agreement—
Agreement to buy goods and sell on consignment.

Consulting Services Agreement—
Defines tasks to be completed by consultant.

Contract—
Basic agreement between two or more parties.

Credit Information Request—
Company request for credit information from potential customer.

Credit Interchange—
Response to request for credit information from another company about a potential customer.

Declaration of Trust—
Trustee's promises to beneficiary regarding property held in trust.

Defective Goods Notice—
Notice to seller of buyer's decision to reject delivery of defective goods.

Demand for Contribution—
One party asks another party to contribute to a payment effected by a contract.

Demand for Delivery—
Buyer demands delivery from seller for goods ordered and paid for.

Demand for Payment—
Creditor's request for payment on past due account.

Demand for Rent—
Landlord's request for tenant to pay rent.

Demand on Guarantor—
Demands that co-signer pay debt.

Demand on Guarantor for Payment—
Creditor's demand for payment from guarantor when debtor defaults.

Demand Promissory Note—
Borrower promises to repay loan upon demand.

Demand to Endorser for Payment—
Cheque or note holder's demand to endorser to pay face amount.

Demand to Pay Promissory Note—
Creditor's demand to debtor to pay note.

Direct Deposit Authorization—
Employee's response to company's request for information about direct deposit payroll.

Disciplinary Notice—
Company's warning to employee regarding behavior.

Dishonored Cheque Placed for Bank Collection—
Company's request to bank to place bad cheque for collection.

Disputed Account Settlement—
Debtor's agreement with creditor about disputed account.

Employee Agreement on Inventions and Patents—
Waiver of employee's rights to any inventions.

Employee Checkout Record—
Supervisor completes upon termination of employee.

Employee Consultation—
Record, and reason for, disciplinary action against employee.

Employee Covenant: Expense Recovery—
Agreement to repay any disallowed expenses.

Employee Exit Interview—
Provides feedback from employee leaving the company.

Employee Indemnity Agreement—
Company agrees to defend employee against negligence or claim of wrongdoing.

Employee Non-Compete Agreement—
Contract to refrain from competing with employer.

Employee Non-Disclosure Agreement—
Contract to keep company information confidential.

Employee Referral Request—
"Thank You" to referring employee.

Employee Release—
Company releases employee from all claims and actions.

Employee Salary Record—
Data and reason for salary increase.

Employee Warning—
Notice of unsatisfactory work performance.

Employee's Agreement on Confidential Data
Employee agrees to be bound by company confidentiality rules.

Employment Agreement—
Terms under which employee agrees to work for company.

Employment Application—
Documents work history, education, and references of applicant.

Employment Application Disclaimer and Acknowledgement—
Authorizes company to verify application.

Employment Changes—
Documents new pay rate for employee.

Exceptions to Purchase Order—
Indicates exclusions to purchase order.

Exclusive Right to Sell—
Agreement giving broker the sole privilege to sell real property.

Exercise of Option—
Written notice of decision to accept option.

Extended Term Rescinded and Demand for Payment—
Notice of default. Entire outstanding balance due within seven days.

Extension of Agreement—
Contract that extends a previous agreement.

Extension of Debt Payment Agreement—
Creditor agrees to new repayment terms.

Extension of Lease—
Contract that extends a previous lease.

Final Notice Before Legal Action—
Letter sent to individual or company with whom you have a dispute.

Final Warning Before Dismissal—
Letter sent to employee as warning prior to termination.

First Warning Notice—
First warning of a company rules violation or unsatisfactory performance.

Funeral Leave Request—
Request for time off to attend a funeral.

General Agreement—
Basic agreement between two or more parties.

General Assignment—
Basic document transferring right and title to a specific item or contract from one person to another.

General Nondisclosure Agreement—
Contract between consultant and client to keep proprietary information secret.

General Subordination—
Creditor agrees to wait behind another creditor.

Grant of Right to Use Name—
Grants one party the right to use the name of another.

Grievance Form—
Gives employee opportunity to voice grievance in writing.

Guaranty—
Third party guarantees payment of another's debts to induce creditor to extend credit.

Guaranty of Rents—
Third party guarantees payment of another's rent to induce landlord to lease.

Help Wanted Advertising Listing—
Information about ad listing.

Illness Report—
Supervisor documents employee's illness.

Incident Report—
Report of incident and action taken.

Indemnity Agreement—
Releases a party from any liability arising from a specific act or transaction.

Independent Contractor Agreement—
Indicates terms of independent contractor's contract.

Information Request on Disputed Charges—
Letter to seller from buyer requesting information on recent charges.

Injury Report—
Supervisor's report of an injury.

Insurance Claim Notice—
Letter to insurance company detailing claim.

Invitation to Quote Price of Goods—
Letter requesting price quote on goods.

Landlord's and Tenant's Mutual Release—
Document that releases both parties from any claims arising from tenancy.

Landlord's Notice to Terminate Tenancy—
Letter to tenant giving notice of landlord's decision to end lease.

Landlord's Notice to Vacate—
Letter specifying date tenant is to vacate premises.

Last Will and Testament—
Sets down the distribution of property upon death.

Lease Termination Agreement—
Mutual agreement to cancel lease before original termination date.

Leave Request/Return From Leave—
Document request for leave and request to return to work.

Letter of Commendation—
Letter commending employee for excellent job performance.

Letter Requesting Authorization to Release Credit Information—
Letter from company to potential customer seeking approval to obtain credit information.

Limited Guaranty—
Third party agrees to a maximum liability of debt for another.

List of Shareholders—
List of shareholders eligible to vote.

Lost Credit Card Notice—
Letter to credit card company from cardholder requesting credit be halted.

—*M*—

Mailing List Name Removal Request—
Letter to company requesting removal of name from mailing list.

Minutes of Annual Meeting of Stockholders—
Record of attendees and proxies.

Minutes of Combined Meeting of Stockholders and Directors—
Records actions of stockholders and directors.

Minutes of Directors' Meeting—
Records actions of directors.

Minutes of First Meeting of Shareholders —
Records actions of shareholders at first meeting.

Minutes of Special Meeting of Stockholders—
Records actions of stockholders at special meeting.

Mutual Cancellation of Contract—
All parties agree to cancel specified contract.

Mutual Releases—
All parties discharge one another from any claim arising from specified contract.

—*N*—

New Employee Data—
Employee's personal information.

No Decision on Hiring—
Letter to applicant explaining that the position will not be filled.

Non-Compete Agreement—
One party agrees not to compete with the business of another.

Non-Disclosure of Trade Secrets—
Applicant agrees not to discuss company trade secrets if hired.

Notice of 30-day Evaluation—
Employee placed on probation for 30 days.

Notice of Annual Shareholders' Meeting—
Notifies shareholders of time, place, and agenda of annual meeting.

Notice of Assignment—
Letter notifying debtor or obligor that account or contract has been transferred to a third party.

Notice of Assignment to Obligor—
Letter notifying obligor of transfer of contract.

Notice of Available Position—
Internal notice regarding new position.

Notice of C.O.D. Terms—
Letter from seller notifying buyer of C.O.D. terms.

Notice of Cash Only Terms—
Notice of C.O.D. shipments only.

Notice of Change in Rent—
Letter from landlord advising tenant of a change in rent.

Notice of Confidentiality Agreement—
Notifies new employer of employee's previous confidentiality agreement.

Notice of Corrected Amount—
Creditor acknowledges its statement is in error.

Notice of Debt Assignment—
Letter to debtor advising of transfer of obligation.

Notice of Default in Payment—
Letter to debtor advising payment is past due.

Notice of Default on Extension Agreement—
Notice that payment has not been received.

Notice of Default on Promissory Note—
Letter to debtor demanding payment and warning of collection.

Notice of Dismissal—
Letter advising employee of company's decision to terminate position.

Notice of Disputed Account—
Letter from customer disputing charges.

Notice of Election to Cancel—
Letter informing party to specified contract of other party's decision to cancel it.

Notice of Forfeiture—
Letter informing party to specified contract of other party's decision to forfeit contract.

Notice of Intent to Repossess Due to Default—
Lender's notice to borrower advising of intent to repossess property effected by default of specified contract.

Notice of Probation—
Employee placed on probation prior to termination.

Notice of Rent Arrears—
Letter advising tenant of past due rent.

Notice of Results of Public Sale—
Letter to debtor stating the outcome of the sale.

Notice of Termination Due to Absence—
Termination due to repeated, unauthorized absences.

Notice of Termination Due to Work Rules Violation—
Letter advising employee of discharge.

Notice of Unpaid Invoice—
Letter to customer detailing payments.

Notice of Waiver of Annual Meeting By All Shareholders—
Waives notice of annual meeting.

Notice of Wrongful Refusal to Accept Delivery—
Letter from seller advising buyer of breach of purchase contract.

Notice to Cancel Back-Ordered Goods—
Letter from buyer advising seller of decision to cancel order for back-ordered goods.

Notice to Cancel Delayed Good—
Letter from buyer advising seller of decision to cancel order because of delay.

Notice to Creditor to Pay Specific Accounts—
Indicates specific invoices to be paid.

Notice to Directors of Special Meeting—
Letter advising directors of special meeting.

Notice to Exercise Lease Option—
Letter from tenant advising landlord of decision to exercise option.

Notice to Landlord to Make Repairs—
Letter advising landlord to repair premises.

Notice to Officer of Removal From Board—
Resolution removing director from the Board of Directors.

Notice to Purchaser of Breach of Option—
Letter from seller advising buyer of violating option terms.

Notice to Reclaim Goods—
Letter from seller advising buyer to return delivered goods.

Notice to Redirect Payments—
Letter informing debtor to pay a third party.

Notice to Re-issue Cheque—
Notice that cheque was never received.

Notice to Remedy Default by Tenant—
Tenant must comply or lease will be cancelled.

Notice to Shareholders of Annual Meeting—
Letter advising shareholders of annual meeting.

Notice to Stop Credit Charge—
Letter from credit cardholder instructing company to withhold payment of specified charge.

Notice to Stop Goods in Transit—
Letter advising shipping company to return goods to seller.

Notice to Tenant to Make Repairs—
Letter from landlord advising tenant to repair premises under terms of lease.

Option to Purchase—
Contract between owner and buyer specifying time period in which to exercise option.

Option to Purchase Stock—
Agreement specifying time period in which to exercise option.

—P—

Partial Shipment Request—
Letter advising buyer of seller's intent to ship a partial order.

Past Due Reminder—
Letter reminding debtor of overdue payment.

Payment Inquiry—
Letter that asks debtor to explain reasons for non-payment.

Payment on Specific Accounts—
Letter specifying to creditor what items shall be paid with enclosed cheque.

Payment on Written Instrument—
Receipt for payment on note's account.

Payments to a Creditor—
Records date and amount of payment, and balance due a creditor.

Permission to Use Copyrighted Material—
Agreement by copyright holder to allow someone to use the copyright.

Permission to Use Quote or Personal Statement—
Agreement granting the use of spoken or written words.

Personal Property Rental Agreement—
Agreement between owner and renter for the use of personal property, for example, a boat.

Personnel Data Change—
Updates employee's personal information.

Personnel Data Sheet—
Documents reason for pay rate change.

Preliminary Employment Application—
Tool for preliminary screening of applicant.

Presentment by Mail—
Demand of payment by mail by the holder of a note.

Privacy Release—
Grants permission to use name, picture, portrait or photograph in all forms of media without prior inspection.

Product Defect Claim—
Letter from wholesaler or retailer advising manufacturer of defect claim.

Product Defect Notice—
Letter from customer advising manufacturer, distributor or seller of a defective product.

Product Warranty Claim—
Letter requesting repair or replacement of defective product under warranty.

Promissory Note—
A promise to pay a principal sum plus interest.

Proposal to Buy a Business—
Letter advising owner of interest in buying business.

Purchase Requirement Agreement—
Contract to purchase a specified quantity of goods during a specific period.

Purchaser's Assignment of Option—
Transfers option rights to a third party.

—R—

Receipt—
Basic receipt for payment that can be used for full or partial payment.

Receipt for Balance of Account—
Used when balance of account is paid.

Receipt for Company Property—
Record of employee accepting responsibility for company property.

Receipt in Full By an Agent—
Used when a third party makes full payment for a debtor.

Receipt in Full by an Agent to an Agent—
Use when a third party representing the creditor accepts full payment from a third party representing the debtor.

Receipt of Note for Collection—
Agent agrees to collect payment on note and retain a percentage for effort.

Receipt on Account for Goods to be Delivered—
Receipt for payment in advance of delivery.

Receipt on Account for Partial Payment —
Receipt for partial payment on account balance.

Reference Report—
Employer's response to request for employee reference.

Release of Breach of Lease by Tenant—
Releases tenant of any liability due to breach of lease.

Release–Individual—
Releases all claims, judgments, demands, actions from one party against another.

Renewal of Notice of Assignment of Accounts—
Notifies interested parties of renewal of transfer of accounts to third party.

Reply to Applicant—
Reply to unsolicited inquiry from student.

Request for Bank Credit Reference—
Letter to bank requesting reference.

Request for Credit Interchange—
Inquiry to another company for credit information on a potential customer.

Request for Information on Overdue Account—
Request for reason for non-payment.

Request for Prepayment—
Creditor denies credit and demands prepayment.

Request for Reference—
Letter to potential employee's previous employer requesting reference.

Request for Transcript—
Applicant's request for school records.

Request to Inspect Personnel File—
Employee's request to inspect own file.

Request to Reduce Balance—
Creditor's request that outstanding balance be reduced.

Residential Rental Application—
Application for rental of residential property.

Resignation—
Resignation letter from employee.

Resume Acknowledgement—
Letter to applicant that resume was received and is under review.

Retirement Checklist—
To do list upon retirement.

Return of Claim as Noncollectible—
Collection agency letter describing failure to collect claim.

Revocation of Guaranty—
Letter notifying creditor of guarantor's decision to revoke guarantee.

—S—

Sale on Approval Acknowledgement —
Letter from seller to buyer admitting goods were shipped for sale on approval.

Sales Representative Agreement—
Contract between company and sales representative to sell company's products or services.

Sample Letter Requesting an Out-of-Court Settlement—
Debtor asks creditor to approve out-of-court settlement.

Sample Letter Requesting Installment Payments—
Debtor proposes to pay in installments.

Samples and Documents Receipt—
Employee acknowledges company samples.

Schedule of Assets for Sale or Loan—
Compares asset, fair market value, and loan value.

Second Notice of Overdue Account—
Letter to debtor requesting payment of past due account.

Second Warning Notice—
Written notice of second rules violation.

Settlement of Disputed Account—
Creditor agrees to settle account for specific sum.

Settlement Offer on Disputed Account—
Creditor offers to settle account for specific sum.

Sight Draft—
An instrument payable upon presentment.

Specific Guaranty—
Agreement by a third party to guarantee the payment of a specific obligation.

Specific Release—
Release from any and all claims, contracts, suits, actions or liabilities specifically arising from a defined act or transaction.

Statement of Wishes—
Document that outlines actions to be taken after a person dies.

Stock Subscription—
Request to purchase shares of a corporation at a given price.

Sublease—
Agreement between tenant, landlord and subtenant to sublet premises currently under lease to tenant that retains tenant's liability.

Summary of Employment Terms—
Summary of initial terms and conditions of employment.

Suspension Without Pay Notice—
Letter to employee to inform him/her of suspension from work without pay.

—T—

Temporary Employment Requisition—
Departmental request for temporary employees.

Tenant's Notice to Exercise Purchase Option—
Letter to landlord accepting option to purchase.

Tenant's Notice to Terminate Tenancy—
Letter advising landlord of decision to cancel lease.

Termination Checklist—
Summary of specific termination requirements.

Termination Letter for Excessive Absenteeism—
Letter of termination due to continued unauthorized absences.

Termination Letter for Intoxication on the Job—
Letter of termination for multiple incidents of on-the-job intoxication.

Time Note—
A promise to pay principal and interest by a specific date.

Transmittal for Collection—
Letter to an attorney requesting collection of an outstanding debt.

Trip Permission—
Authorizes minor to take a trip and appoints an adult to render medical care if necessary.

—U—

Unsolicited Idea Acknowledgement—
Company's reply to receiving idea.

—V—

Verification of Education—
Employer's request to verify education of potential employee.

Verification of Employment—
Employer's confidential recommendation of former employee.

Verification of Licensure—
License holder's request for verification of registration.

—W—

Waiver and Assumption of Risk—
Customer's agreement to hold seller harmless from any liability or risk in using product or service.

Waiver of Liability—
Notice to reschedule meeting.

Waiver of Notice of Annual Meeting by Individual Shareholder—
Stockholder's release of corporation from required meeting notice.

Waiver of Notice of Directors' Meeting—
Director's release of corporation from required meeting notice.

Waiver of Notice of Organization Meeting of Incorporators and Directors—
Incorporators' and directors' release of corporation from required meeting notice.

Waiver of Notice—Combined Meeting—
Shareholder/director waives notice of meeting.

Warranty Bill of Sale—
Documents sale of property warrantied with good and marketable title.

Withheld Delivery Notice—
Letter advising buyer of reasons seller has not delivered goods.

Written Unanimous Consent in Lieu of Meeting—
Corporate document that provides stockholder approval of action without meeting.